The World's Greatest
HOTELS
RESORTS
+ SPAS

A terrace
at J.K. Place,
on Capri.

TRAVEL
+LEISURE

The World's Greatest
HOTELS
RESORTS
+SPAS

FOURTH EDITION

TRAVEL
+LEISURE
BOOKS

AMERICAN EXPRESS PUBLISHING CORPORATION, NEW YORK

TRAVEL + LEISURE
THE WORLD'S GREATEST HOTELS, RESORTS, + SPAS
FOURTH EDITION

Project Editors Laura Begley, Irene Edwards,
Peter Jon Lindberg, Meeghan Truelove
Art Director Leigh Nelson
Production Manager David Richey
Photo Editor Robyn Lange
Assistant Book Editor Alison Goran
Reporters Catesby Holmes, Mario López-Cordero,
Meg Lukens Noonan, Suzanne Mozes, Kathryn
O'Shea-Evans, Madhu Puri, Maria Shollenbarger
Copy Editors Stephen Clair, David Gunderson, Diego
Hadis, Jane Halsey, Mike Iveson, Ellie Sweeney
Researchers Marya Spence, Bradford Taylor

TRAVEL + LEISURE

Editor-in-Chief Nancy Novogrod
Creative Director Nora Sheehan
Executive Editor Jennifer Barr
Deputy Editor Laura Begley
Managing Editor Mike Fazioli
Arts/Research Editor Mario R. Mercado
Copy Chief Lee Magill
Photo Editor Katie Dunn
Production Director Rosalie Abatemarco-Samat
Production Manager Ayad Sinawi

AMERICAN EXPRESS
PUBLISHING CORPORATION

President, C.E.O. Ed Kelly
S.V.P., Chief Marketing Officer Mark V. Stanich
C.F.O., S.V.P., Corporate Development & Operations
Paul B. Francis
V.P., General Manager Keith Strohmeier, Frank Bland
V.P., Books & Products, Publisher Marshall Corey
Director, Book Programs Bruce Spanier
Senior Marketing Manager, Branded Books Eric Lucie
Assistant Marketing Manager Lizabeth Clark
Director of Fulfillment & Premium Value Phil Black
Manager of Customer Experience & Product
Development Charles Graver
Director of Finance Tom Noonan
Associate Business Manager Desiree Bernardez
Corporate Production Manager Stuart Handelman

Cover design by Leigh Nelson
Front cover: Fort on Fisher's Pan, Onguma Game
Reserve, Namibia; photographed by David Rogers.
Back cover, from left: The pool at Amankila, in Bali,
Indonesia; photographed by Darren Soh. A guest
room at The Landing, on Harbour Island, in the
Bahamas; photographed by Brooke Slezak. The
manor house at Quinta do Vallado, in Portugal's
Duoro Valley; photographed by David Nicolas.

ISBN 978-0-7566-4282-2 | ISSN 1559-0372

Published by American Express
Publishing Corporation
1120 Avenue of the Americas
New York, New York 10036

With Contributions and Distributed
by DK Publishing, Inc.
375 Hudson Street, New York, New York 10014
Manufactured in China

The Rimps tea
lounge, at Taj
Tashi, in Bhutan.

CONTENTS

Tierra Atacama
Hotel & Spa,
in Chile.

KEY TO THE PRICE ICONS   **$** UNDER $250   **$$** $250–$499   **$$$** $500–$749   **$$$$** $750–$999   **$$$$$** $1,000 AND UP

A guest room at Banyan Tree Lijiang, in China's Yunnan Province.

A courtyard at
Si Said, part of
Angsana Riads
Collection,
in Marrakesh,
Morocco.

The beachside pool at Anjajavy l'Hôtel, in Madagascar.

INTRODUCTION

We have always paid special—some might say obsessive—attention to hotels at *Travel + Leisure*, seeing them not merely as places to refuel and retreat from the world, but also as a reflection of the world around them. Where we stay tells us much about where we are. That is a central premise of T+L's fourth annual compendium of the hotels and resorts that define travel now. *Travel + Leisure* profiles thousands of hotels in the course of a single year; our editors combed through 12 months' worth of issues to select the 122 highlights you'll find here. We also present the results of the World's Best Awards, T+L's annual survey of our readers' favorites. In the back of the book, we've compiled a user-friendly section of directories that lets you search for properties by location and category.

Taken together, the properties within this book point to some encouraging trends:

Eco-friendliness remains a priority. Even in such unlikely locales as China and Mozambique, many of this year's standouts make a big impact with a minimal footprint.

Reuse, recycle, reinvent. Hotel developers are ingeniously reworking existing properties—from a maharajah's palace in Jodhpur to a landmark jail in Boston.

A new globalism is afoot. Architects, designers, and hotel chefs are mixing international styles with flair. How very 21st-century that a boutique hotel in Hong Kong pays homage to Salvador Dalí; that Gordon Ramsay's food is served at the new Hilton in Prague; and that Egyptian artifacts adorn a lobby in Barcelona.

Intimate is the new outsize. The latest generation of hotels function more like private homes or pieds-à-terre: properties like Paris's five-room Hôtel Particulier Montmartre, hidden down a secret passage; or Angsana Riads, a collection of seven luxurious single-family houses in Marrakesh.

Access is key. Whether through exclusive arrangements or simply an expert concierge desk, the best properties grant their guests entrée to unique experiences and sights, making even first-time visitors feel like insiders.

Travel can transform. Hotels are helping to renew unsung neighborhoods, cities, even whole regions. A number of destinations are appearing here for the first time—places like Thimphu, Bhutan; Iznájar, Spain; and San Juan del Sur, Nicaragua. The traveler's map is constantly evolving and expanding, and hotels play a decisive role in how that map unfolds.

We hope these pages will inspire new journeys and expand your own map of the world.

By Nancy Novogrod, *Editor-in-Chief*

A guest room
at the Tides South
Beach, in Miami.

UNITED STATES + CANADA

THE WAUWINET

NANTUCKET, MASSACHUSETTS

At the end of the 19th century, this stately shingled inn provided hearty dinners and a decent night's lodging to sea-weary whalers. Today the kitchen serves poached lobster with sweet-ricotta tortellini and black-truffle foam, and rooms are gussied up with pine antiques and classic prints. But the warm welcome is the same. Staff outnumber guests three to one and organize everything from romantic sunset picnics and surf-casting sessions to afternoon port and cheese in the parlor. All good options—if you can bear to leave that wicker lounge chair set on the expansive grounds between the Atlantic and Nantucket Harbor.

120 Wauwinet Rd., Nantucket, Mass.; 800/426-8718 or 508/228-0145; wauwinet.com; doubles from $$$

The Nantucket Harbor–facing lawn at the Wauwinet.

LIBERTY HOTEL

BOSTON, MASSACHUSETTS

It sounds like a setup for a joke: "A landmark Boston jailhouse is converted into a luxury hotel..." While the just-opened Liberty Hotel does indulge in all the requisite penitentiary puns—room service is "solitary dining," the bar is in the former basement drunk tank—it's more than the sum of its gimmicks. The best feature is the stone cruciform building itself, designed in the 1840's by Gridley J. F. Bryant in the austere Boston Granite style. With contemporary interiors by Alexandra Champalimaud, a restaurant run by Lydia Shire, and a prime location near Beacon Hill, the Liberty makes an excellent place for a weekend furlough.

215 Charles St., Boston, Mass.; 866/507-5245 or 617/224-4000; libertyhotel.com; doubles from $$$

The Liberty Hotel's
90-foot-tall atrium.

17

ROYALTON

NEW YORK, NEW YORK

When Ian Schrager and Steve Rubell opened the Royalton in 1988, the aesthetic was pure flash and theatricality. Two decades later, the hotel has been reimagined by the sharp design firm Roman & Williams. Dazzle has given way to depth, cool vibes to coziness. A vintage Venini chandelier lights the 105-foot-long hallway that divides the intimate spaces of the slate-floored lobby. Suede-upholstered sofas line slatted walls; a monumental double-sided fireplace provides a warm focal point. The wood-paneled restaurant serves updated bistro classics (roast chicken au jus, pan-seared *branzino*) as unlikely to go out of style as the Royalton itself.

44 W. 44th St., New York, N.Y.; 800/635-9013 or 212/869-4400; royaltonhotel.com; doubles from $$$

The Royalton's lobby. Opposite: Stephen Alesch and Robin Standfer, of design firm Roman & Williams, by the central fireplace.

GREENWICH HOTEL

NEW YORK, NEW YORK

With two restaurants, a cinema, and a film festival to his credit, Robert De Niro is one of TriBeCa's most influential tastemakers. His Next Big Thing: the 88-room Greenwich Hotel, a tour de force of pitch-perfect eclecticism (a Louis XVI–style bed is paired with a velvet Beaumont & Fletcher sofa; Tibetan silk rugs set off English leather settees). The drawing room's enormous multifaceted ceiling lights hail from a Horn & Hardart Automat, one of New York's iconic working-class cafeterias—a nice touch from *the* iconic taxi driver.

377 Greenwich St., New York, N.Y.; 212/941-8900; thegreenwich hotel.com; doubles from $$$

A guest room at the Greenwich Hotel. Opposite: Robert De Niro at the entrance to the hotel's courtyard.

SURF LODGE

MONTAUK, NEW YORK

Owned by a team of New York City club impresarios, the Surf Lodge made a high-profile splash when it opened in Montauk, a formerly scruffy Long Island enclave now one-upping the Hamptons with its relaxed sense of style. Interiors are minimalist and beachy, with hanging rattan basket chairs, sea-themed artwork, and teak bowls turned into sinks. *Top Chef* star Sam Talbot helms the restaurant, and surfer movies play 24/7 in the lobby. After dark, the open-air deck doubles as the area's hottest nightspot.

183 Edgemere St., Montauk, N.Y.; 631/668-2632; thesurflodge.com; doubles from $$, two-night minimum

Outside the Surf Lodge's Tracy Feith store.

The Rondeau cabin's bedroom, at Lake Placid Lodge.

LAKE PLACID LODGE

LAKE PLACID, NEW YORK

WORLD'S BEST

Like the Great Camps that flourished here more than a century ago, Lake Placid Lodge reflects the grandeur of its Adirondack Mountain setting. This former fishing outpost opened in 1882 and was recently restored after a 2005 fire. But the lodge's best assets are the 19 luxe lakeshore cabins from the 1920's and 1930's, which pamper guests with near-invisible service. A breakfast of raspberry pancakes and house-made preserves arrives magically in a wicker basket, then is whisked away when you're not looking; blanket-strewn Adirondack chairs form a circle around the fire pit at dusk, with gourmet fixings for s'mores on a table nearby.

Whiteface Inn Rd., Lake Placid, N.Y.; 877/523-2700 or 518/523-2700; lakeplacidlodge.com; doubles from $$$$, including breakfast and afternoon tea

The lobby at the
Donovan House,
designed by
Studio Gaia.

DONOVAN HOUSE

WASHINGTON, D.C.

The latest venture from the Thompson Hotel group is named after "Wild" Bill Donovan, nonconformist father of the CIA—fitting for a property whose design is a bold departure for Washington, D.C. The lobby features bowl-shaped chairs that hang from the ceiling and exaggerated wingback loungers; rooms have leather-paneled walls and cocoon-like, spiral-shaped showers. But the teak-floored roof, with its pool, cocktail lounge, and potted cherry trees, seals the deal, making the hotel a coveted hideout for politicos.

1155 14th St. NW, Washington, D.C.; 800/383-6900 or 202/737-1200; thompsonhotels.com; doubles from $$

TIDES
SOUTH
BEACH

MIAMI BEACH, FLORIDA

Miami has been a city of big, brash hotels since the 1950's. Although the landscape is always changing, a few properties rise above the rest, including South Beach's Tides. The Art Deco icon was recently overhauled by design star Kelly Wearstler, whose Palm Beach–revisited treatment includes a sunset palette and lots of blond wood. Faux tortoise shells festoon the Mediterranean-inspired restaurant; the lobby's marble bar top is French. In the guest rooms, chair backs are carved to resemble leaves, and whimsical table lamps have bases shaped like conch shells. Wearstler's clever take on organic ocean-house style creates a space where guests can feel comfy *and* fabulous.

1220 Ocean Dr., Miami Beach, Fla.; 800/439-4095 or 305/604-5070; tidessouthbeach.com; doubles from $$$

One of two
poolside cabanas
at the Tides.

A Gansevoort
South suite.

GANSEVOORT SOUTH

MIAMI BEACH, FLORIDA

When the owners of the Hotel Gansevoort, in New York's clubby
Meatpacking District, set out to create their next property, they
didn't want a carbon copy. The new venture has Manhattan-style
amenities (David Barton gym; Big Drop boutique) and unabashed
Miami appeal: its rooftop lounge, Plunge—a sprawling, over-the-
top playground—features chandelier-lit cabanas, a 110-foot-long
pool, palm trees, and a granite bar. But the highlight is the view:
to the west, the city skyline; to the east, the vast Atlantic.

2377 Collins Ave., Miami Beach, Fla.; 305/604-1000; gansevoortsouth.com;
doubles from $$$

Azul del Mar's façade, below. Left: A view of the grounds and the beach.

AZUL DEL MAR

KEY LARGO, FLORIDA

Just south of the Everglades is the six-room Art Deco villa Azul del Mar. The property is decidedly quiet, thanks to its secluded beach and adults-only policy. Book the Garden Suite Caribe, for its Jacuzzi-jet bathtub and private patio. The Aquamarina and Celeste rooms, with floor-to-ceiling windows and views of Florida Bay, tie for second place. Snorkel in nearby John Pennekamp Coral Reef State Park, which includes part of North America's largest living reef, or settle into an oceanside chaise longue to watch pods of dolphins and flocks of migrating birds, not to mention fabulous sunsets.

104300 Overseas Hwy., Key Largo, Fla.; 888/253-2985 or 305/451-0337; azulhotels.us; doubles from $

HOTEL SAN JOSÉ

AUSTIN, TEXAS

In the up-and-coming South Congress district, across the street from the club where Stevie Ray Vaughan got his start, lies the Hotel San José. The 1938 Spanish colonial–style motel has gone from seedy to chic: rooms are dressed up with crisp paisley textiles and Bertoia-inspired chairs. Take one of the hotel's bicycles to nearby Ladybird Lake, or kick back in the manicured courtyard with a longneck of Shiner (a local brew) and a Joplin-loaded iPod.

1316 S. Congress Ave., Austin, Tex.; 800/574-8897 or 512/444-7322; sanjosehotel.com; doubles from $

Room 54 at the Hotel San José. Opposite: The ivy-covered entrance to the Courtyard building.

Tivoli Lodge
owner Bob
Lazier, above.
Above right: The
hotel's Alps-
inspired exterior.

TIVOLI LODGE

VAIL, COLORADO

Serious skiers have long been drawn to Vail's vast bowls and wide-open slopes, but the town itself was in a decades-long deep freeze—until now. The mountainside hamlet is in the midst of what's been dubbed the Billion-Dollar Renewal, a wave of redevelopment that includes the $30 million basement-to-roof shingles rebuild of the Tivoli Lodge. Constructed in 1968 by owners Bob and Diane Lazier, two happy-go-lucky ski bums, the 62-room hotel has kept its Tyrolean feel but added digital-age comforts: computer-controlled lighting systems, Swedish walk-in showers with body jets, wireless access throughout the entire hotel. Rooms in the northwest-facing tower have sweeping views—from the Gore Range to glittering Vail village.

386 Hanson Ranch Rd., Vail, Colo.; 800/451-4756 or 970/476-5615; tivolilodge.com; doubles from $$

The Montana-flagstone fireplace in the Hotel Terra's lobby.

HOTEL TERRA

JACKSON HOLE, WYOMING

The new alpine-luxe, LEED-certified Hotel Terra—one mile from Grand Teton National Park and ski-in distance from Jackson Hole Mountain—mixes low-impact ethics with high-end aesthetics. Specially coated floor-to-ceiling windows regulate heat flow and showcase stunning views; plush towels and robes are made of fair-trade organic cotton. The mod-Western lobby features sleek reclaimed-wood tables—more proof of how far eco-friendly design has come.

3335 W. Village Drive, Teton Village, Wyo.; 800/631-6281 or 307/739-4000; hotelterrajacksonhole.com; doubles from $

NOFTSGER HILL INN BED & BREAKFAST

GLOBE, ARIZONA

The Apache Trail is a 40-mile route that curves east from Phoenix past towering saguaros. At its end lies the Noftsger Hill Inn Bed & Breakfast, a 1907 former schoolhouse overlooking the historic mining town of Globe. Rooms come with Mission-style rockers, fringed Victorian lampshades, locally stitched quilts, and original blackboards—complete with chalk for commentary and doodles.

425 North St., Globe, Ariz.; 877/780-2479 or 928/425-2260; noftsgerhillinn. com; doubles from $

The Mexican Fiesta room at Noftsger Hill Inn Bed & Breakfast.

ARIZONA INN

TUCSON, ARIZONA

Tucson's health-conscious visitors can check in to any number of spa resorts, but since 1930, those in search of glamour have headed straight for the Arizona Inn. Palm-lined brick paths slice a brilliant green lawn, then wend through mazelike gardens to pink adobe-style casitas with George Catlin lithographs and Hepplewhite sideboards. Poolside dining and the jazz pianist at the 1917 Steinway in the Audubon Bar will make you feel like a guest from Hollywood's golden age.

2200 E. Elm St., Tucson, Ariz.; 800/933-1093 or 520/325-1541; arizonainn.com; doubles from $$

One of the Arizona Inn's original casitas.

A newly revamped room at the Flamingo. Opposite: A vividly reimagined hallway.

FLAMINGO LAS VEGAS

LAS VEGAS, NEVADA

As glitzy new towers kept bumping classic hotels off the Vegas map, locals predicted doom for the Flamingo, opened by mobster Bugsy Siegel in 1946. Instead, its owner, Harrah's, decided to redo 1,032 guest rooms in an exuberant tribute to the hotel's original look. Vinyl headboards rise ceiling-high; fresh carpets are a riot of green, chocolate, and pink. The maximalism continues on the 27-acre grounds, with waterslides, three free-form lagoons, and patrols of flamingos and black-necked swans.

3555 Las Vegas Blvd. S., Las Vegas, Nev.; 800/732-2111 or 702/733-3111; flamingolasvegas.com; doubles from $

HOTEL DEL CORONADO

CORONADO, CALIFORNIA

WORLD'S BEST Sepia photographs of bowler-hatted crowds on the boardwalk hang in the lobby of the Hotel del Coronado, attesting to the 120-year-old hotel's deep history. (Every U.S. president since LBJ has stayed here.) The sprawling Victorian landmark is a California icon; recently the Del added the Beach Village, 78 rooms in 11 oceanside villas that can be configured as two- or three-bedroom units, each with a full kitchen and many with a fire-pit–equipped patio. With its own entrance, the compound feels like a low-key country club, secreted away from the bustle of the main hotel.

1500 Orange Ave., Coronado, Calif.; 866/433-3030 or 619/522-8811; delbeachvillage.com; villas from $$$$

On the beach in front of the Del.

A guest room at the Thompson Beverly Hills.

THOMPSON BEVERLY HILLS

BEVERLY HILLS, CALIFORNIA

Manhattan hotelier Jason Pomeranc couldn't have picked a more incongruous spot—a former Best Western—for his third West Coast outpost. But at the Thompson Beverly Hills, the Dodd Mitchell–designed interiors (vertical smoked mirrors; chocolate leather walls; spherical chrome lamps) have a 70's-style bachelor-pad flair. Glossy black, dimly lit hallways showcase oversize Steven Klein photographs. The rooftop pool has peepholes along its sides. After dark, the scene revolves around the open-air nightspot, ABH, which serves up sushi from the hotel restaurant, Bond Street, alongside a 360-degree panorama of L.A.

9360 Wilshire Blvd., Beverly Hills, Calif.; 800/441-5050 or 310/273-1400; thompsonhotels.com; doubles from $$

One of 97 guest rooms at the Canary Hotel. Opposite: The rooftop lounge.

CANARY HOTEL

SANTA BARBARA, CALIFORNIA

The owners of the Canary Hotel helped define SoCal luxury at Santa Monica's Shutters on the Beach and Casa del Mar, and their latest retreat captures the same breezy glamour. L.A. designer Michael Smith created an Alhambra-meets-Pacific aesthetic: terra-cotta floors and tapestries in the lobby, turquoise hallways set off by Moroccan lanterns, and an 1,800-square-foot rooftop terrace with a pool, two fireplaces, and views of the Santa Ynez Mountains.

31 W. Carrillo St., Santa Barbara, Calif.; 877/468-3515 or 805/884-0300; canarysantabarbara.com; doubles from $$

Sierra Mar, the
restaurant at the
Post Ranch Inn,
with views of
Big Sur. Opposite:
A Pacific suite.

POST RANCH INN

BIG SUR, CALIFORNIA

On central California's craggy Pacific coast, the Post Ranch Inn has reinvented the notion of the bungalow. The resort's structures resemble refined tree houses, each with a fireplace and enormous windows. In 2008, the hotel added six sprawling suites, designed as intersecting glass-walled rooms that reveal sea and sky but keep you hidden from other guests. Staff can arrange a yoga session or guided walk through redwood forests. Another equally enticing possibility: whiling away the hours on your private porch, surveying a scene so awe-inspiring, you can read the curve of the earth in the ocean.

Hwy. 1, Big Sur, Calif.; 800/527-2200 or 831/667-2200; postranchinn.com; doubles from $$$, including breakfast

ACE HOTEL

PORTLAND, OREGON

This is pure Portland: creative, authentic, irreverent. Rooms in the revamped 1912 hotel are decorated with murals and fitted with vintage claw-foot tubs; bedside tables are fashioned from secondhand tomes (the famous Powell's Books is just down the block). It's no wonder bands on tour like to stay here: there are in-room turntables and vintage LP's, and guitar strings for sale at the front desk. Staff dressed in Nom de Guerre–conceived ensembles (button-down shirts, crisp Dickies pants) are as cool as the surroundings.

1022 SW Stark St., Portland, Oreg.; 503/228-2277; acehotel.com; doubles from $

The Ace Hotel's wood-paneled lobby. Opposite: Room No. 308, with a mural by Portland artist Scrappers.

Inside a guest tent at Clayoquot Wilderness Resort.

CLAYOQUOT WILDERNESS RESORT

BEDWELL HARBOUR, BRITISH COLUMBIA

"Roughing it" at Clayoquot should appeal to even the most dedicated sybarite. A floatplane brings guests from Vancouver to a secluded compound hugging a spruce- and cedar-shaded shore. The 20 antiques-furnished tents have fireplaces and birchwood beds piled high with down comforters and pillows. Hearty four-course dinners are prepared with regional ingredients—free-range hens, small-batch cheeses, just-picked berries. After kayaking the nearby fjords, head to the waterfront wood-fired hot tub, keeping an eye out for blue herons and harbor seals.

Bedwell Harbour, B.C.; 888/333-5405 or 250/726-8235; wildretreat.com; doubles from $$$$$, three-night minimum, all-inclusive

WICKANINNISH INN

TOFINO, BRITISH COLUMBIA

WORLD'S BEST The Wickaninnish Inn, set on a remote, pine forest–ringed promontory, is best enjoyed during fierce weather—the more ferocious, the better. In the 75 rooms, duvet-covered beds and deep soaking tubs sit beside floor-to-ceiling windows that look out on the churning ocean and rain-lashed coast. Don a slicker for a walk on Chesterman Beach, or snuggle up next to your fireplace with a Pacific Northwest Pinot Noir and the binoculars that are provided in each room.

500 Osprey Lane, Tofino, B.C.; 800/333-4604 or 250/725-3100; wickinn.com; doubles from $$

The Wickaninnish Inn's restaurant, the Pointe, overlooking the Pacific.

Looking out at
North Sound
from a guest-room
balcony at the
Bitter End Yacht Club,
on Virgin Gorda.

CARIBBEAN + THE BAHAMAS

A villa pool at the Four Seasons Resort Nevis.

FOUR SEASONS RESORT NEVIS

CHARLESTOWN, NEVIS

WORLD'S BEST The Leeward Island of Nevis (population: 11,000) is tiny and untouristed, without a high-rise hotel or traffic light in sight. Its highlight: the Four Seasons, where gingerbread-trimmed cottages fan out around a prime stretch of four-mile-long Pinney's Beach. Rooms feature marble baths, mahogany furniture, and cheerful floral prints, but the pièce de résistance is the resort's spa. Tucked into a garden blooming with poinciana trees are 12 treatment rooms and a waterfall plunge pool. Earn your mango-and-sea-salt body scrub on the Robert Trent Jones II–designed golf course—or with a hard day's loll beneath an umbrella by the sea.

Charlestown, Nevis; 800/332-3442 or 869/469-1111; fourseasons.com; doubles from $$$

Montpelier Plantation Inn's 16-seat restaurant, inside a former sugar mill.

MONTPELIER PLANTATION INN

ST. JOHN'S PARISH, NEVIS

A stay at Montpelier Plantation Inn is so comfortable it almost feels like a visit to a friend's house—if that house were a refined tropical estate, where butlers unpack and press your clothes. Nineteen rooms are scattered through nine low-slung buildings on this former sugar estate; each has a veranda and louvered windows looking out on the slopes of Mount Nevis. Cocktails are served in the fieldstone great house, dinner on the terrace or in a converted 18th-century mill. Don't miss the locally caught mahi-mahi, roasted in plantain leaves and sprinkled with brown sugar harvested on the property.

St. John's Parish, Nevis; 869/469-3462; montpeliernevis.com; doubles from $$$

Sol é Luna's Coco
Tiare suite,
above. Above
right: The
pathway leading
to the pool.

SOL É LUNA INN

MONT VERNON, ST. MARTIN

Bougainvillea-draped Sol é Luna is hidden
away in a residential neighborhood on French
St. Martin's north end, halfway between ceru-
lean Orient Bay and Grand Case, a fishing
village filled with cafés. Each of the six rooms
delivers an updated twist on rustic Provençal
style. Check in to Nacre for its private palm-
shaded whirlpool, or the Mango, painted in
warm shades of yellow and coral. After exploring
the island's beaches and hiking trails, you'll
be more than ready for chef Christian Moreau's
dishes, such as olive-crusted halibut, phyllo-
wrapped lamb, and roast duck with mango.

Mont Vernon, St. Martin; 590-590/290-856; soleluna
restaurant.com; doubles from $

QUEEN'S GARDENS RESORT

TROY HILL, SABA

A wooded, five-square-mile dormant volcano crossed by a thin, winding road, Dutch-controlled Saba is one of the most unspoiled islands in the Caribbean. Not for beachgoers—it is virtually sand-free—Saba lures nature lovers and divers with its rain-forest hiking trails and superb protected reefs. Queen's Gardens Resort is tucked in a grove of mango trees at the base of Mount Scenery. The 12 airy suites are furnished with British and Dutch Colonial antiques, plus modern touches like flat-screen TV's and iPod docks. By day, the outdoor lounge offers picture-perfect views of the hills and the sapphire sea. By night, tiki torches light the pathways surrounding the island's largest pool.

Troy Hill, Saba; 599/416-3494; queenssaba.com; doubles from $$

The pool at the Queen's Gardens Resort.

One of the
Bitter End Yacht
Club's new
Barbara Hulanicki-
designed guest
rooms. Opposite:
On a villa porch,
overlooking
the water.

BITTER END YACHT CLUB

VIRGIN GORDA, BRITISH VIRGIN ISLANDS

Watersports are the focus at this easygoing resort. Guests get unlimited use of more than 100 vessels—Sunfish, windsurfers, motorboats—and a sailing school helps budding skippers learn their jibs from their jibes. Daily excursions include deep-sea fishing, scuba diving, and sightseeing at the nearby Baths, an iconic jumble of boulders that frame clear pools. The nautical vibe is enhanced by transient charter boaters who come ashore to dine under the fluttering yacht flags of the open-air restaurant. Long-awaited renovations have just been completed: the original beach villas now sport bright blue-and-orange fabrics and teak furniture designed by Barbara Hulanicki. Happily, the roomy porches, with their inviting hammocks, are unchanged.

North Sound, Virgin Gorda, BVI; 800/872-2392; beyc.com; doubles from $$$$, all-inclusive

BIRAS CREEK

VIRGIN GORDA, BRITISH VIRGIN ISLANDS

On a secluded and hilly 140-acre peninsula, Biras Creek feels like its own world. Guests arrive by boat or helicopter and are whisked off in a golf cart to one of the cottage suites— each of which has an outdoor shower and a pair of bicycles parked at the entryway. A short stroll past a salt-pond bird sanctuary is Deep Bay, where you'll find a trove of catamarans, kayaks, and Boston Whalers for guests to use. To truly escape, untie one and zip along the scrubby coastline until you spy the perfect cove to call your own for the day.

Berchers Bay, Virgin Gorda, BVI; 877/883-0756 or 284/494-3555; biras.com; doubles from $$$$$, including meals

A bedroom in one of Biras Creek's oceanside villas.

The central living room at Hacienda Gripiñas.

HACIENDA GRIPIÑAS

JAYUYA, PUERTO RICO

Hidden at the end of a bumpy side road off Puerto Rico's scenic Ruta Panorámica, the tin-roofed Hacienda Gripiñas, built in 1858 as the homestead of a wealthy plantation owner, still evokes that graceful way of life. Mountain breezes drift in through shutter-framed windows, keeping the small sitting rooms cool. Some of the clapboard-wall guest quarters have verandas overlooking the spring-fed pool; Adirondack-chair rockers dot the public terraces. Follow one of the walking trails into the surrounding hills, thick with coffee plants, banana trees, and bird-of-paradise blossoms. And don't miss the inn's excellent *carne guisada,* a traditional beef stew made with tomatoes and pigeon peas.

Estatal, Jayuya, Puerto Rico; 787/828-1717; haciendagripinas.com; doubles from $, including meals

HORNED DORSET PRIMAVERA

RINCÓN, PUERTO RICO

Spread over seven acres that tumble down to the Caribbean on Puerto Rico's western coast, the Horned Dorset Primavera is the height of laid-back tropical luxe. Decorated in Spanish colonial style, the buildings are whitewashed stucco with clay-tile roofs, ringing a lush central courtyard complete with a terra-cotta fountain. The 39 suites are artfully furnished with Balinese mahogany furniture, North African pendant lamps, antique botanical prints, and ceiling fans with blades fashioned from palm leaves. Unlike the throngs of oceanside resorts that tout dizzying lists of nonstop activities, the Horned Dorset prides itself on its lack of distractions. Stroll the isolated beach, enjoy chef Aaron Wratten's celebrated Nuevo Latino cooking (crab-and-coconut chowder, tamarind-glazed pork loin with *mofongo*), then climb into your four-poster bed and be lulled to sleep by the waves lapping just beyond the French doors.

Km 3, Crta. 429, Rincón, Puerto Rico; 800/633-1857 or 787/823-4030; horneddorset.com; doubles from $$$

One of the Horned
Dorset Primavera's
six new suites.
Opposite: Chef Aaron
Wratten in the
main dining room.

59

Goldeneye's
three-bedroom
Royal Palm villa.
Opposite: The
living room of
Ian Fleming's
former residence.

GOLDENEYE

ORACABESSA, JAMAICA

The estate where Ian Fleming created James Bond is now a resort owned by Island Records founder Chris Blackwell—and is still the type of place where a weary sophisticate might come to recharge, martini in hand. Curled around a lagoon, the cliff-top main house and four cottages are hidden in a jungle of cannonball trees and tall African tulips; interiors are filled with bamboo furniture and bright batiks. Guests have exclusive use of nine Jet Skis and a glass-bottomed boat. The beach is secret enough for a meeting of MI6, and each butler-serviced villa is a paean to privacy: ideal for a tryst with that spy who loves you.

Oracabessa, Jamaica; 800/688-7678 or 876/975-3354; goldeneyehotel.com; doubles from $$$$, all-inclusive

Inside one of
Tiamo's 11 guest
bungalows, above.
Above right:
The white-sand
pathway leading
from the dining
room to the beach.

TIAMO

SOUTH ANDROS ISLAND, BAHAMAS

This solar-powered hideaway, set alongside a
pristine stretch of sand on largely undeveloped
South Andros Island, uses less electricity per
month than one average American household.
And it has other green cred, too: deep wrap-
around porches that shield the colorful guest
cottages from the sun and keep interiors cool;
a bank of small refrigerators in place of an
energy-hungry kitchen walk-in. There's a ban
on unsustainably harvested seafood (including
local catches, like conch). Staff biologists lead
excursions to the island's natural wonders,
including the Blue Holes, underwater caves
first explored by Jacques Cousteau.

Driggs Hill, South Andros Island, Bahamas; 242/369-2330;
tiamoresorts.com; doubles from $$$$, including meals

The Landing's Attic room, which has views of the harbor.

THE LANDING

HARBOUR ISLAND, BAHAMAS

The seven-room Landing has a decidedly patrician vibe. The hotel was conceived by Tracy Barry (whose mother was the first-ever Miss Bahamas) and Toby Tyler, a Sydney restaurateur. India Hicks—daughter of the iconic 60's designer David Hicks, great-great-granddaughter of Queen Victoria, and bridesmaid to Diana, Princess of Wales—spearheaded the interiors. Her childhood holidays on Eleuthera helped her hit just the right tone, with crisp Ralph Lauren linens and classic plantation-style beds designed by her partner, David Flint Wood. There are no televisions or phones to distract you, only the periodic docking of the ferry at the small pier across the street.

Dunmore Town, Harbour Island, Bahamas; 242/333-2707; harbourislandlanding.com; doubles from $$

The retro-chic
lounge bar
at Pink Sands.

PINK SANDS

HARBOUR ISLAND, BAHAMAS

Since it opened in 1951, this resort has occupied an enviable spot on Harbour Island's famously rose-hued beach, and its guest book has been signed by the likes of Richard Gere, Diane von Furstenberg, and Mick Jagger. The property has changed hands several times over the years, but its draws still include 25 sea-themed villas set among winding, palm-lined gardens, a pink-edged, free-form pool, and a stylish main lodge kitted out with carved-wood furnishings and tinkling seashell chandeliers.

Chapel St., Harbour Island, Bahamas; 800/407-4776 or 242/333-2030; pinksandsresort.com; doubles from $$$$

The 19th-century courtyard at Melville Suites, in Mazatlán, Mexico.

MEXICO +
CENTRAL +
SOUTH
AMERICA

Mandarin Oriental Riviera Maya's main pool. Opposite: The reception area in the open-air lobby.

MANDARIN ORIENTAL RIVIERA MAYA

PLAYA DEL CARMEN, MEXICO

It's official: The Riviera Maya, a once-sleepy string of beaches 40 miles south of Cancún, has arrived. Witness the recent opening of Mandarin Oriental, whose winning formula—great service, forward-thinking design, a posh spa—has been transported to a pristine coastal environment, with acres of mangrove forest fringing a petite stretch of sand. The 128 boxy white villas have polished stone floors, rough limestone walls, sculptures by prominent Mexican artists, and water views. Add to that four restaurants and a rooftop bar, and you've got the most sophisticated resort on Yucatán's ever-evolving eastern coast.

Km. 298.8, Carr. Federal Cancún, Playa del Carmen, Mexico; 800/526-6566 or 52-984/877-3269; mandarinoriental.com; doubles from $$$

CASASANDRA HOTEL

HOLBOX, MEXICO

The island of Holbox (pronounced "*Ole*-bosh") is a tiny spit of land off the Yucatán Peninsula, laced with sand roads. As soon as Cuban-born artist Sandra Pérez arrived, she knew she wanted to stay for good, so she created a retreat that would feel more like a residence than a formal hotel. CasaSandra, the 20-room result, is spread out among seven oceanfront buildings decorated with Guadalajaran antiques and brightly colored hand-woven linens. Palapas are sprinkled along the beach, and the water's edge is 50 uninterrupted steps away. Ask the staff to arrange a fishing excursion, then have chef Mariela Rajo prepare your catch for dinner. From June to August, you can swim alongside harmless migrating whale sharks.

Calle de la Igualdad, Holbox, Mexico; 52-984/875-2431; casasandra.com; doubles from $$

Palapas line the Gulf of Mexico at CasaSandra.

The pool at Camino Real, right. Below: One of the hotel's 91 guest rooms.

CAMINO REAL

OAXACA, MEXICO

Originally a Dominican convent built in 1576, the Camino Real is filled with history. Bougainvillea spills over the cloister archways; a stone basin where nuns once laundered their habits is now a courtyard fountain. Indoors, guest rooms have ebony-hued antique beds and terra-cotta tiled ceilings, with 16th-century frescoes covering some of the walls. At the restaurant, El Refectorio, sample one of seven variations on the classic mole, the regional specialty made from ground chiles, chocolate, and nuts.

300 Calle Cinco de Mayo, Oaxaca, Mexico; 800/722-6466 or 52-951/501-6100; camino-real-oaxaca.com; doubles from $$, including breakfast, three-night minimum

Melville Suites' D. H. Lawrence room. Opposite: The courtyard, with a fountain crafted from local volcanic stone.

MELVILLE SUITES

MAZATLÁN, MEXICO

During the late 19th century, Mazatlán was a playground for well-traveled artists and aristocrats. Today their Neoclassical mansions are being transformed into stylish cafés, galleries, and hotels. The most vibrant reinvention is Melville Suites, an inn that occupies a former nunnery in the town's historic center. Monastic austerity has been replaced by a profusion of lively details in the 20 suites: steamer-trunk tables, billowy curtains, and hand-carved armoires. On the walls, colorful works by area artists prove that the seaside town still inspires.

99 Avda. Constitución, Mazatlán, Mexico; 52-669/982-8474; themelville.com; doubles from $, including breakfast

EL SILENCIO LODGE & SPA

BAJOS DEL TORO, COSTA RICA

Costa Rica has long been a favorite destination for the rugged backpacking set, but until recently there have been few resort options for the well-heeled crowd. Enter El Silencio: 16 cottages scattered across 500 acres in the mountainous Bajos del Toro region. An activities concierge leads excursions to waterfalls and tree-canopy ziplines, but many guests choose to simply stay put—despite the lack of in-room TV's, cell-phone reception, or Internet hookups. Each bungalow has an outdoor whirlpool set high above the cloud-wreathed forest, a place to sit and realize that sometimes *silencio* is the greatest luxury of all.

Bajos del Toro, Costa Rica; 866/446-4063 or 011-506/2291-3044; elsilenciolodge.com; doubles from $$, all-inclusive

On a lookout deck of a guest cabin at El Silencio.

MORGAN'S ROCK HACIENDA & ECO-LODGE

SAN JUAN DEL SUR, NICARAGUA

Most guests heading to this thatched-roof resort near La Flor National Park pack hiking boots and swimsuits, anticipating the area's tropical forests and Pacific Coast beaches. But some also bring books to donate to the school that Morgan's Rock helps support. The lodge is blazing a trail in Central America's green-tourism industry with its do-the-right-thing ethos. Cathedral ceilings are crafted from responsibly harvested woods; nature guides are recruited from surrounding villages. Kayak through mangroves as the sun rises, then tuck into almond pancakes and juice squeezed from fruit grown in the property's own gardens.

Playa Ocotal, San Juan del Sur, Nicaragua; 506-2/232-6449; morgansrock.com; doubles from $$$, including meals

The poolside restaurant, La Bastide, at Morgan's Rock.

LA LANCHA

TIKAL, GUATEMALA

Francis Ford Coppola's latest resort fits seamlessly into the surrounding jungle. Ten thatched-roof casitas hug a steep hillside overlooking the blue, island-sprinkled expanse of Lake Petén Itzá. Rooms are stylish and comfortable, furnished with Guatemalan antiques and hand-dyed, locally woven textiles. After admiring the lake and rain forest from the hammock on your private deck, get a closer look on a sunrise boat tour or from the nearby jungle-canopy "skywalk." The highlight of your stay: a special guided outing to Tikal, the largest ancient Mayan site ever discovered.

Lago Petén Itzá, Tikal, Guatemala; 800/746-3743 or 011-501/824-4912; blancaneaux.com; doubles from $

La Lancha's bi-level swimming pool.

Republican Patio, a restaurant at Charleston Cartagena. Opposite: The men's spa lounge.

CHARLESTON CARTAGENA

CARTAGENA, COLOMBIA

Travelers in the know are once again flocking to Cartagena for its architecture, beaches, and white-hot nightlife. The Charleston Cartagena is the city's grand dame: the sweeping staircases and hand-painted woodwork of the original building, a 17th-century convent, have been preserved; the 90 guest rooms are outfitted with marble bathrooms and flat-screen TV's, with views of the leafy courtyard, walled Old Town, or Caribbean Sea. The rooftop infinity pool looks out onto 300-year-old cupolas and brand-new skyscrapers, and the plaza in front of the hotel is a lively gathering spot. Retreat from the action with a coffee-and-maté facial at the hotel spa.

31-23 Carr. 3A, Centro Plaza de Santa Teresa; Cartagena, Colombia; 57-5/664-9494; hotelescharleston.com; doubles from $$, including breakfast

The patio and pool at El Marqués.

EL MARQUÉS

CARTAGENA, COLOMBIA

In Cartagena's cobblestoned Old Town, El Marqués Hotel still feels like an old colonial home. Ornate wooden balconies look out over courtyards and shaded terraces, rustic beams and polished stone floors set off white walls and bathrooms, and low-slung canvas chairs create quiet nooks under the palms. La Cava, the hotel's restaurant, is one of the town's best, with outdoor seating by a fountain and dishes like snapper *à la plancha* with avocado mousse.

33-41 Calle Nuestra Señora del Carmen, Cartagena, Colombia; 57-5/664-4438; elmarqueshotelboutique.com; doubles from $$, including breakfast

Hotel Monasterio's
Baroque entryway.

HOTEL MONASTERIO

CUZCO, PERU

In the Andean capital of Cuzco, this 1595 onetime Jesuit seminary—a relic of early Spanish colonial architecture—has been transformed by Orient-Express Hotels. The 126 guest rooms, former monks' cells, are dressed up with antiques and 18th-century paintings. The Baroque chapel houses an impressive collection of religious art. Order an excellent pisco sour from the barrel-vaulted lobby bar while a harpist in traditional dress provides the accompaniment.

136 Calle Palacios, Plazoleta Nazarenas, Cuzco, Peru; 800/237-1236 or 51-84/604-000; orient-express.com; doubles from $$$

The pool and main building at Chile's Tierra Atacama. Opposite: The hotel's restaurant.

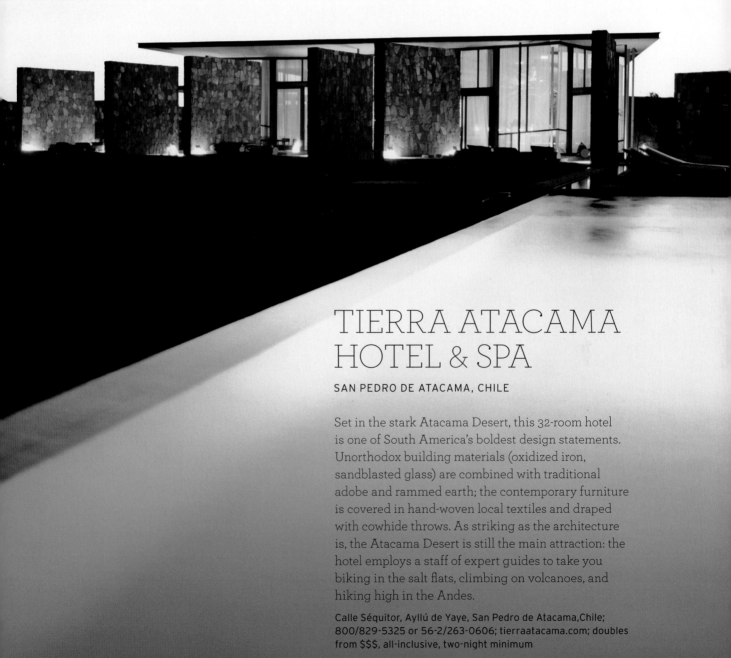

TIERRA ATACAMA HOTEL & SPA

SAN PEDRO DE ATACAMA, CHILE

Set in the stark Atacama Desert, this 32-room hotel is one of South America's boldest design statements. Unorthodox building materials (oxidized iron, sandblasted glass) are combined with traditional adobe and rammed earth; the contemporary furniture is covered in hand-woven local textiles and draped with cowhide throws. As striking as the architecture is, the Atacama Desert is still the main attraction: the hotel employs a staff of expert guides to take you biking in the salt flats, climbing on volcanoes, and hiking high in the Andes.

Calle Séquitor, Ayllú de Yaye, San Pedro de Atacama, Chile; 800/829-5325 or 56-2/263-0606; tierraatacama.com; doubles from $$$, all-inclusive, two-night minimum

EXPLORA EN RAPA NUI, POSADA DE MIKE RAPU

EASTER ISLAND, CHILE

With the opening of Explora's 30-room lodge, Easter Island finally has a hotel befitting its landscape. The LEED-certified property—set on 23 acres between the Pacific Ocean and a massive volcano—takes its inspiration from the surrounding environment. Buildings are constructed from native woods and rock, and interiors are chic but spare. Only residents are allowed to build on the remote isle, so hotelier Pedro Ibañez partnered with free-diving champion Mike Rapu (who gave the hotel its quirky name). Guides lead trips to natural pools, yawning craters, and, of course, to see the island's famed *moai* statues.

Easter Island, Chile; 866/750-6699 or 56-2/206-6060; explora.com; doubles from $$$$, all-inclusive, three-night minimum

Explora's
curved exterior.
Opposite: A guest
room overlooking
the Pacific.

Correntoso Lake & River Hotel's lobby. Opposite: The lodge, on the edge of Lake Nahuel Huapí.

CORRENTOSO LAKE & RIVER HOTEL

VILLA LA ANGOSTURA, ARGENTINA

On a bluff overlooking Lake Nahuel Huapí, Correntoso Lake & River Hotel started life almost a century ago as a cabin for fly fishermen pursuing the area's legendary trout. Anglers still come, though the lodge's original rusticity has been refined: there's now an herbal hammam and a wine list that features bottles of Malbec from Argentina's top producers. Interiors combine cozy comforts—beds piled high with duvets, sink-in-to-your-shoulders tubs—with details that reflect the hotel's forest setting, including exposed wood paneling and a stone fireplace lit with a roaring fire.

Ruta de los Siete Lagos y Rio Correntoso, Villa la Angostura, Argentina; 54-11/4803-0030; correntoso.com; doubles from $$, including breakfast

87

The Cocker's salon, with its wall of eclectic art.

THE COCKER

BUENOS AIRES, ARGENTINA

Set in San Telmo—a Buenos Aires district that's rapidly revitalizing—the four-room Cocker is aristocratic yet homey, traditional yet full of surprises. An old pull-lever cash register, straight from the nearby antiques market, sits at the reception desk; guests get a copy of a hand-annotated (and invaluable) neighborhood map. Hotel staff have personally vetted every café and restaurant recommended, and the suggestions extend right down to the type of house wine you should order at the nearby *parrillas* to avoid a morning headache.

458 Juan de Garay, Buenos Aires, Argentina; 54-11/4362-8451; thecocker.com; doubles from $, including breakfast

A guest room
at Rio's new
Hotel Fasano.

HOTEL FASANO

RIO DE JANEIRO, BRAZIL

Restaurateur Rogério Fasano established himself as
a tastemaker par excellence with his five-year-old Hotel
Fasano São Paulo. Its new sister, in Rio's stylish Ipanema,
is equally hot and seductive. The Philippe Starck–
designed interiors have a Midcentury Modern vibe:
yellow onyx lamps, leather-upholstered Mies daybeds,
tree stump–inspired tables. The result embodies
laid-back Carioca chic, right down to the Havaianas
flip-flops that are standard-issue in each room.

80 Avda. Vieira Souto, Rio de Janeiro, Brazil; 55-21/3202-4254;
fasano.com.br; doubles from $$$

A guest room at Le Delos, on France's Île de Bendor.

EUROPE

The Haymarket's
conservatory.
Opposite: The
pool, lit by a
Martin Richman
installation.

HAYMARKET HOTEL

LONDON, ENGLAND

"Why not have some fun!" may well have been what Kit Kemp said as she released her arsenal of bold colors and supergraphic effects on the public spaces of the former American Express London headquarters in the heart of the theater district. Masters of the clubby/cozy/contemporary (including one of our all-time favorites, the Charlotte Street Hotel), the designer and her husband and business partner, Tim Kemp, create memorable public spaces. Even the Haymarket's indoor pool lounge is no mere fitness center—its wenge-and-pewter bar, nightclub-caliber sound system, and 300-person capacity are clearly meant for after-hours activities.

1 Suffolk Place, London, England; 44-20/7470-4000; haymarkethotel.com; doubles from $$

The Knightsbridge
Hotel's room No. 301.

KNIGHTSBRIDGE HOTEL

LONDON, ENGLAND

The look is traditional English contemporary—bold patterns and plumped-up
pillows meet granite-and-oak bathrooms and sandstone fireplaces—at this
44-room hotel on a quiet cul-de-sac in tony Knightsbridge, a stone's throw from
Harrods. Snug parlors and a well-stocked honor bar add to the appeal. Regular
refurbishments by co-owner and designer Kit Kemp—each year two rooms are
made over completely—keep the place feeling fresh.

10 Beaufort Gardens, Knightsbridge, London, England; 800/553-6674 or 44-20/7584-6300;
knightsbridgehotel.com; doubles from $$

HOPE STREET HOTEL

LIVERPOOL, ENGLAND

A once-dreary waterfront city recently dubbed a European Capital of Culture, Liverpool has always prided itself on being out of the mainstream. The Hope Street Hotel is in the Georgian Quarter, near several repertory theaters. The 48 rooms in the converted furniture store are spare and airy, and warmed by polished radiant-heat floors; exposed century-old brick walls are set off by crisp white linens. The restaurant in the 19th-century carriage works downstairs is one of Liverpool's best—try sage-rubbed veal with Puy lentils or Scottish salmon with potted shrimp.

40 Hope St., Liverpool, England; 44-151/709-3000; hopestreethotel.co.uk; doubles from $$

A corner room at the Hope Street Hotel, featuring a cherrywood bed.

The Malmaison, with the Port of Liverpool building in the background.

MALMAISON

LIVERPOOL, ENGLAND

The glass-and-steel Malmaison is a flashy addition to the banks of the Mersey. A shiny industrial metal stairway spirals upward at the front desk to the champagne bar; architectural photographs of the city help set the urbane mood. Rooms are dark-toned, with gauzy black curtains and leather furniture accented by plum-colored pillows. Explore historic dockyards and museums just steps from the hotel.

7 William Jessop Way, Princes Dock, Liverpool, England; 44-151/229-5000; malmaison.com; doubles from $

The glittering lobby of the Radisson SAS Royal Hotel.

RADISSON SAS ROYAL HOTEL

DUBLIN, IRELAND

Located on the quiet stretch of Golden Lane between St. Patrick's Cathedral and Temple Bar, the new Radisson SAS Royal is perfect for design-forward business travelers. The open-plan lounge and bar gleam with panels of glossy wood and marble; the dramatic central staircase is wrapped in glass etched with text from the Irish Constitution. All 150 rooms have flat-screen TV's and vast rain showers, and even the standard-issue gray carpeting is kicked up a notch with streaks of fuchsia.

Golden Lane, Dublin, Ireland; 800/333-3333 or 353-1/898-2900; radissonsas.com; doubles from $

A guest room at
the Dylan Hotel,
above. Above right:
The hotel's lantern-
lined entrance.

DYLAN HOTEL

DUBLIN, IRELAND

The stately red-brick Victorian exterior provides
little hint of what's inside. The public spaces
are downright trippy—a bar covered in black-
and-red faux Fortuny wallpaper, a library with
stark white club chairs set on an acid-green rug.
But the spacious guest rooms are slightly more
restrained, with a cream and brown palette
and headboards designed by Christopher Guy.
The linens are Frette, Etro amenities line the
bathroom sinks, and closets are stocked with
extra comforts. The wide terrace, dotted
with deep armchairs, low tables, and glass
lanterns, is the ideal spot for predinner drinks.

Eastmoreland Place, Dublin, Ireland; 353-1/660-3000;
dylan.ie; doubles from $$, including breakfast

RITZ-CARLTON POWERSCOURT

COUNTY WICKLOW, IRELAND

A half-hour drive from central Dublin, the 18th-century Powerscourt manor is perhaps the loveliest and most visited working estate in the British Isles. The 200 guest rooms, in a newly constructed building, have eiderdown-swathed beds and marble-clad bathrooms with heated floors. Forty-four acres of formal gardens are a five-minute walk away. The pub serves up a rib-sticking menu and has excellent beers on tap—though the real high-fliers, who choose to arrive on the hotel's helicopter landing pad, may opt for the Gordon Ramsay restaurant.

Powerscourt Estate, Enniskerry, County Wicklow, Ireland; 800/241-3333 or 353-1/274-8888; ritzcarlton.com; doubles from $$, including breakfast

The Ritz-Carlton Powerscourt's Palladian-style façade.

Relaxing by Casa
Rural el Olivar's
pool, surrounded
by orange trees.

CASA RURAL EL OLIVAR

IZNÁJAR, SPAIN

Iznájar is the quintessential *pueblo blanco,* a whitewashed village
rising from the hills of Andalusia. Two Belgian expats recently opened
the five-room Casa Rural el Olivar, a former farm on the town's
outskirts. Furnishings are minimal, resourceful, and stylish: roof tiles
repurposed as sconces, crown canopies crafted from yards of white
linen. The wicker chaise longues by the infinity pool are perfectly
positioned for views of a sapphire lake and acres of olive trees.

6 Cierzos y Cabreras, Iznájar, Spain; 34/95-753-4928; casaruralelolivar.com;
doubles from $

The lobby at Hotel Claris.

HOTEL CLARIS

BARCELONA, SPAIN

Housed in the 19th-century Palacio Vedruna, one block from the bustling Passeig de Gràcia, Hotel Claris combines the timeless with the cutting-edge: a three-story steel-and-glass addition tops the original ornate structure. Rooms are decorated with antique kilims and Napoleonic engravings, as well as rich accents of unexpected color; the small but sleek rooftop pool is reached via futuristic glass elevators. The highlights: a lobby display of ancient Egyptian artifacts and original Marilyns by Andy Warhol in the hotel restaurant.

150 Pau Claris, Barcelona, Spain; 800/525-4800 or 34/90-233-7294; derbyhotels.es; doubles from $$$

The Igeldo room
at Hotel Iturregi.
Opposite: The pool.

HOTEL ITURREGI

GETARIA, SPAIN

This eight-room property, set in the hilly vineyards outside the tiny fishing village of Getaria, makes an ideal under-the-radar base from which to explore Spain's Basque coast. Interiors are cool and subdued, with the occasional boldly patterned fabric or surprising combination (a sharp-angled love seat next to a Louis XVI–style bench). Venture 15 miles east to Spain's modern culinary mecca, San Sebastián.

Barrio Azkizu, Getaria, Spain; 34/94-389-6134; hoteliturregi.com; doubles from $$, including breakfast

103

QUINTA DA ROMANEIRA

COTAS, PORTUGAL

A stay at Quinta da Romaneira, a 1,000-acre riverside wine estate with two renovated manor houses, has the vibe of an elaborate house party. Every meal is set in a different location—on a terrace shaded by lemon trees, in a firelit library. The original port cellar has been converted into a pool and hammam (a subtle nod to Portugal's Moorish era), and the storehouse is now a chocolate factory where tea cakes and creamy fudge are served every afternoon. At turndown, a staff member appears at your door bearing a glass of delicate white port.

Cotas, Portugal; 351-25/473-2432; maisondesreves.com; doubles from $$$$$, all-inclusive

Inside Quinta da Romaneira's salon. Opposite, from far left: The estate's guesthouses; the indoor pool, in an old port cellar.

105

QUINTA DO VALLADO

PESO DA RÉGUA, PORTUGAL

Sixth-generation winemaker João Ferreira Álvares Ribeiro converted part of his family's 18th-century manor into five simple but comfortable guest rooms, with painted headboards and shuttered doors that open onto a gravel path. The estate straddles the Corgo River, and visitors are free to explore—canoes for navigating between the banks are provided. The adjacent farmhouse includes an informal drawing room and a new demonstration kitchen, where Ribeiro pairs the estate's young wines with Portuguese dishes such as *rojões* (stewed pork with potatoes).

Vilarinho dos Freieres, Peso da Régua, Portugal; 351-25/432-3147; quintadovallado.com; doubles from $, including breakfast

The manor at Quinta do Vallado.

The lobby at Le Meurice.

LE MEURICE

PARIS, FRANCE

Philippe Starck's redo of this Paris institution, including its Michelin three-starred restaurant, features some surreal touches, from table legs shod in fancy footwear to a frosted mirror (it's literally refrigerator-cooled). But there's still plenty of tradition, such as the green and white marble floors in the lobby that were restored by Italian craftsmen. For such chic digs, the Meurice is surprisingly family-friendly, loaning children custom-made boats to sail on the pond in the nearby Tuileries.

228 Rue de Rivoli, First Arr., Paris, France; 800/650-1842 or 33-1/44-58-10-10; lemeurice.com; doubles from $$$$

HÔTEL PARTICULIER MONTMARTRE

PARIS, FRANCE

The five-room Hôtel Particulier Montmartre, on a leafy cobblestoned passageway, is a pint-size hideaway with outsize design. The three-story Directoire façade is pleasingly geometrical—lead urns march up the steps to the front door, which is framed by iron lanterns on brackets. But the artist-designed rooms add unexpected edge. One is wrapped in a photomural of dense branches. Another is dressed entirely in men's suiting fabrics: a *drap de laine* bedcover edged in tuxedo satin, pin-striped flannel for a buttoned slipper chair. The garden, full of plush little pockets of evergreen shrubs and trees, is by celebrity landscape designer Louis Benech, who made it feel wild and impromptu—just barely brought to heel.

23 Junot Ave., 18th Arr., Paris, France; 33-1/53-41-81-40; hotel-particulier-montmartre.com; doubles from $$$

The bath area of the Tree with Ears room, at Paris's Hôtel Particulier Montmartre, above. Above left: The Curtain of Hair room. Opposite: The hotel's entrance.

Château Les Merles's pool and grounds. Opposite: The hotel's Neoclassical exterior.

CHÂTEAU LES MERLES

DORDOGNE, FRANCE

Part of France's new wave of country hotels and restaurants, this estate dates from 1677, with a 19th-century château built by one of Napoleon's generals. Dutch decorator Joris van Grinsven plays off Les Merles's Neoclassical bones with simple, but not spartan, style. A crisp palette of white slipcovered sofas, charcoal-gray throws, and ebony-stained floors comes alive with a few ornate flourishes—Louis XV chairs covered in magenta velvet, gilt-framed mirrors. There's a nine-hole golf course and a formal dining room serving foie gras terrine and turbot *en papillote* with an impressive list of Bergerac wines.

Tuilières, Mouleydier, Dordogne, France; 33-5/53-63-13-42; lesmerles.com; doubles from $

LE DELOS

ÎLE DE BENDOR, FRANCE

A monument to the endearingly loopy vision of pastis magnate Paul Ricard (who built it in 1962), the 19-room Le Delos was recently reimagined by British designer Carolyn Quartermaine, who brought cohesion to the eccentric mix. Thronelike armchairs are re-covered in vintage bedsheets dyed pink; linens are printed with fragments of 17th-century calligraphy; artist Didier Mahieu's drawings are sketched directly on bedroom walls. Happily, the best of Ricard's beloved frippery (vivaciously colored tiles, allegorical mosaics, wrought-iron schooner chandeliers) still remains.

Île de Bendor, France; 33-4/97-05-90-90; bendor.com; doubles from $$

The salon at Le Delos. Opposite: Didier Mahieu wall drawings in a guest room.

Château de
Germigney's pool.

CHÂTEAU DE GERMIGNEY

JURA, FRANCE

A rugged but serene paradise that stretches from Burgundy to Switzerland, the Jura is home to lakes, gorges, hills, and the Château de Germigney, a recently renovated 18th-century manor. Set in a manicured park with well-tended English gardens and linden allées, the former marquis's residence has 21 guest rooms with wide cedar planks and yards of toiles and rich silks—a perfect spot for sampling the area's pleasures. Sip the local golden *vin jaune* with nutty Comté cheese in the formal restaurant. For dinner outdoors, amble into the village, where the hotel runs a riverside bistro.

Rue Edgar Faure, Port-Lesney, Jura, France; 33-3/84-73-85-85; chateaudegermigney.com; doubles from $

LES PALMIERS

ST.-TROPEZ, FRANCE

Ever since Brigitte Bardot vacationed on these shores, St.-Tropez has been the French Riviera's most glamorous destination. But for guests on less than a movie-star budget, Les Palmiers, a three-story house set in a thicket of tropical trees, has 25 cheerful, affordable rooms. The king-size beds and bright Provençal prints are low-key and comfortable, and breakfast is served under the palms on the hotel's garden terrace.

24-26 Blvd. Vasserot, St.-Tropez, France; 33-4/94-97-01-61; hotel-les-palmiers.com; doubles from $

The 19th-century Les Palmiers.

One of Room National's two suites.

ROOM NATIONAL

ANTWERP, BELGIUM

Check into Violetta and Vera Pepa's petite B&B, and a smiling sister will show you to the gold leaf–filled double room (tiny and sexy) or one of two airy suites. Croissants, fresh fruit, and strong coffee await outside your door each morning. This is a great value in Antwerp, with an Old City location that couldn't be better for checking out the design capital's fashion scene. The pioneering ModeMuseum (home to a Yohji Yamamoto store) is just down the street, adjacent to Dries van Noten's Modepaleis.

24 Nationalestraat, Antwerp, Belgium; 32-3/226-0700; roomnational.com; doubles from $, including breakfast

CLARION
HOTEL SIGN

STOCKHOLM, SWEDEN

The country behind Ikea brings a similarly streamlined aesthetic to the affordable hotel chain Clarion. Designed by Gert Wingårdh, this outpost has an exterior that features noiseproof granite facing the railroad and sheer glass fronting lovely Norra Bantorget park. All 558 rooms are furnished with the work of Scandinavia's top 20th-century masters, such as Bruno Mathsson and Hans Wegner. Best of all, Swedish star Marcus Samuelsson, the chef at New York's Aquavit, has opened a restaurant here.

35 Östra Järnvägsgatan, Stockholm, Sweden; 46-8/676-9800; clarionsign.com; doubles from $$

Clarion Hotel
Sign's eighth-floor
champagne bar,
with Eero Aarnio
Bubble Chairs.

CHARLES HOTEL

MUNICH, GERMANY

Designed by architect and native son Christoph Sattler (who helped redevelop Berlin's Potsdamer Platz), the Charles Hotel was inspired by the Belle Époque hotels of the Côte d'Azur. In the rotunda lobby, portraits by 19th-century Munich painter Franz von Lenbach are hung above crescent-shaped banquettes in velvet and faux snakeskin. Book a room overlooking the old botanical gardens or splurge on the presidential Monforte suite, which has its own steam room and grand piano.

28 Sophienstrasse, Munich, Germany; 800/667-9477 or 49-89/544-5550; roccofortecollection.com; doubles from $$$

The Charles Hotel's Italian restaurant, Daverro. Opposite: The Monforte suite's study.

121

The lobby at Hilton Old Town.

HILTON OLD TOWN

PRAGUE, CZECH REPUBLIC

For its recent multimillion-dollar, top-to-bottom overhaul, the Hilton Old Town assembled a team of Europe's finest talent. Designer Alexandra Champalimaud introduced a contemporary vibe and a saffron and taupe palette to the 305 rooms, while David Collins used a graphic motif inspired by Czech Modernist art in the public spaces. And the man responsible for the hotel's Maze restaurant, which serves dishes like pressed foie gras and poached chicken with fig marmalade: celebrity chef Gordon Ramsay.

7 V Celnici, Prague, Czech Republic; 800/445-8667 or 420-2/2484-2364; doubles from $$

Palais Coburg's Bastion Garden, where guests can eat dinner alfresco.

PALAIS COBURG

VIENNA, AUSTRIA

Built atop the old walls of Vienna in the 1840's, the former summer residence of Ferdinand von Saxe-Coburg-Gotha was turned into a hotel in 2003. The erstwhile palace is divided into 35 suites, each decorated in one of two styles: traditional (original moldings, grand swagged curtains) or contemporary (glass walls, angular furniture). The grounds make the hotel feel peaceful and removed, but all of Vienna's top attractions—shopping, opera, museums—are just minutes away.

4 Coburgbastei, Vienna, Austria; 800/735-2478 or 43-1/518-180; palais-coburg.com; doubles from $$$

Schloss Velden's
1890 château
and, across the
formal lawn,
its new annex.

SCHLOSS VELDEN

VELDEN, AUSTRIA

On the edge of Lake Wörth, in a pocket of the Carinthia region known as the Austrian Riviera, Schloss Velden has lived many lives. It began in 1603 as a manor house and was rebuilt in 1890 as a turreted château. In 2007, Horst Schulze, the former vice chairman of Ritz-Carlton and the head of upstart luxury brand Capella Hotels & Resorts, turned the mansion into a 39-room hotel, adding a Jabornegg & Palffy–designed, glass-walled annex for another 66 rooms. He's on to something: rain-forest showers, double-sided fireplaces, Pratesi linens, and a private assistant who phones guests ahead of time to make sure they get anything they want. Macrobiotic food? Pillows stuffed with fresh mint leaves? These are not empty promises.

1 Schlosspark, Velden, Austria; 877/247-6688 or 43-4274/520-000; schlossveldencapella.com; doubles from $$$

Badrutt's Palace
Hotel's lobby,
overlooking the
Alps. Opposite:
The Grand Hall's
marble corridor.

BADRUTT'S PALACE HOTEL

ST. MORITZ, SWITZERLAND

A throwback to the days of glamorous schussing followed by tuxedo-and–evening gown dinners, Badrutt's Palace is still the center of high-society socializing in St. Moritz. A black and white marble corridor, the Grand Hall, extends the length of the lobby, from the grand dining room at one end to the clubby lounge at the other, where St. Moritz fixture Mario da Como has tended bar and told stories since 1963. Interiors have been overhauled—marble tubs in rooms, a glass façade for the indoor pool—and a new outpost of Nobu is another nod to the jet-set scene.

27 Via Serlas, St. Moritz, Switzerland; 800/745-8883 or 41-81/837-1000; badruttspalace.com; doubles from $$$

A hallway at Il Cannito, with paintings by Italian artist Pietro Lista.

IL CANNITO

PAESTUM, ITALY

South of the Amalfi Coast's thronged piazzas lies Italy's still-undiscovered Cilento Coast. The best place from which to explore it: Il Cannito, a four-bedroom inn opened in 2006 by Anna Maria Borlotti Gorga, a chef from the area, and her family. The two 13th-century buildings have rough-hewn, whitewashed beams, contemporary paintings, and flat-screen TV's. Guests can sunbathe and swim at the Gorgas' private lido on the beach, just beyond the Greek temples at Paestum. The sound system is usually tuned to reggae or West African music—a perfect background track for sipping a glass of crisp Falanghina.

Via Cannito, Paestum, Italy; 39-0828/196-2277; ilcannito.com; doubles from $$, including breakfast

RELAIS & CHÂTEAUX IL FALCONIERE

CORTONA, ITALY

Wine tastings, a 2,500-square-foot spa, and tours of nearby towns are just a few of the reasons to visit this restored-villa estate, located on a 25-acre vineyard outside Arezzo. The 20 guest rooms are housed in the original manor, in the farmhouse, or next to the chapel; the airy *limonaia* is now a world-class restaurant. Sign up for a class in traditional Tuscan or Cortonese cooking, complete with visits to area markets.

370 Località San Martino, Cortona, Italy; 800/735-2478 or 39-05/7561-2679; ilfalconiere.it; doubles from $$

Part of the 17th-century Tuscan manor at Il Falconiere.

Hotel Cala di Volpe's
seawater pool
and restaurant.
Opposite: A corner
of the lobby bar.

HOTEL CALA DI VOLPE

SARDINIA, ITALY

Located on the Costa Smeralda, one of the most exclusive spots in the Mediterranean, the Hotel Cala di Volpe was built 40 years ago by the Aga Khan. The limestone compound, modeled after a fishing village, has porticos, archways, turrets, and 124 whitewashed, pastel-accented rooms. Power broker guests and anchored yachties meet on the patio for an elaborate buffet dinner that's booked solid all summer long.

Porto Cervo, Costa Smeralda, Sardinia, Italy; 800/325-3589 or 39-078/997-6111; luxurycollection.com; doubles from $$$$$, all-inclusive

J.K. Place Capri, housed in a 19th-century villa. Opposite: The bar and breakfast room.

J.K. PLACE CAPRI

CAPRI, ITALY

A rare seaside hotel in Capri, J.K. Place is charming and mellow, slightly removed from the island's crowds. The vibe is nautical with a twist: porthole-shaped interior windows, sea blue walls, crisp white sofas. Parquet floors and chandeliers add a dash of formality—yet guests have complete run of the house. Pick chiles in the garden to sprinkle on your pasta at lunch, then sip Bellinis on the terrace as you watch the bathers on the beach below.

225 Via Provinciale Marina Grande, Capri, Italy; 39-081/838-4001; jkcapri.com; doubles from $$$, including breakfast

The restaurant at Mystique, a hotel carved out of volcanic rock.

MYSTIQUE

SANTORINI, GREECE

Built into the cliffs overlooking Santorini's
Aegean-filled caldera, Mystique isn't fully
visible from the road. But descend about 30
steep stone stairs and you'll discover sea-facing
terraces, alfresco dining nooks, and an infinity
pool. In Mystique's 18 rooms, local materials
(limestone floors, driftwood headboards) and
naturalistic forms (curved and sloping walls,
egg-shaped tables) create an otherworldly
effect, along with window views that look like
a mirage. Check in, catch the sunset from
your private patio, then wander over to the
wine cellar—a 150-year-old cave—for a tasting.

Oia, Santorini, Greece; 800/325-3589 or
30-22/8607-1114; mystique.gr; doubles from $$$$

Herders' hats from the Fulani tribe, on display at South Africa's Madikwe Safari Lodge.

AFRICA + THE MIDDLE EAST

FORT ON FISHER'S PAN

ONGUMA GAME RESERVE, NAMIBIA

Northern Namibia is Africa's next great safari frontier—in part because of its wildlife, but also because of its wealth of luxury lodges, such as this camp on a private 50,000-acre game reserve five minutes from Etosha National Park. The Fort on Fisher's Pan takes the bush outpost in a bold new direction, with carved antique doors, reflecting pools, and Moroccan-inspired lanterns—almost as if a casbah had been relocated to southern Africa. Each guest room has two canvas walls that open to reveal the thornbush-dotted savanna, part of a unique, sprawling preserve rich with salt deposits that attract a menagerie of creatures.

Onguma Game Reserve, Namibia; 264-61/232-009; onguma.com; doubles from $$$, all-inclusive

The pool deck and open-air lounge at the Fort on Fisher's Pan.

Pezula's champagne and whiskey bar.

PEZULA RESORT HOTEL & SPA

KNYSNA, SOUTH AFRICA

Three hundred miles from Cape Town, this exclusive getaway (tennis superstar Roger Federer bought a private residence here) is set on a bluff above the ocean. Part of an expansive development that also includes an 18-hole golf course, horse stables, and villas, the 78 suites are clean-lined and airy, with contemporary South African art. The restaurant, Zachary's, is one of the finest in the Cape area (try the guava-barbecued quail or free-range Namibian beef). The polo fields of Plettenberg Bay are only a helicopter transfer away.

Lagoon View Dr., Knysna, South Africa; 27-44/302-3333; pezularesorthotel.com; doubles from $$$

A communal sitting room at Madikwe Safari Lodge.

MADIKWE SAFARI LODGE

MADIKWE GAME RESERVE, SOUTH AFRICA

When Madikwe Game Reserve was established in 1991, the 185,000 acres were virtually bereft of wildlife. Today, after rigorous conservation efforts, the preserve teems with elephants, leopards, and giraffes—and the 20-suite Madikwe Safari Lodge is right in the middle of it all. The intimate three-camp complex highlights design guru Chris Browne's pared-down aesthetic with natural stonework and tree-trunk frames. The thatched-roof stone huts have private plunge pools; dinner is served in the communal open-air *boma* or on your candlelit private deck. The nightly ritual: glasses of iced *mampoer*, a traditional Afrikaner eau-de-vie, at sundown by the Marico River.

Madikwe Game Reserve, South Africa; 888/882-3742; andbeyond.com; doubles from $$$$$, all-inclusive

BOESMANSKOP

OUDTSHOORN, SOUTH AFRICA

An unlikely desert utopia is blossoming in South Africa's Karoo region—artists and other creative urbanites have fled the cities for the revitalized villages along these dusty roads and mountain passes. In Oudtshoorn, a town in the Swartberg Mountain foothills, Tinie Bekker has transformed part of his family's ancestral farm into a two-bedroom inn with Victorian claw-foot tubs, antique South African armoires, and jungle-thick gardens of agapanthus and iris. He calls the style "rustic Cape Country Afrikaner." Ask Bekker to cook for you: using ingredients procured from neighbors and his own garden, he turns out delectable dishes like Karoo-pastured lamb roast and organic fig pie.

R62, Oudtshoorn, South Africa; 27-44/213-3365; boesmanskop.co.za; doubles from $, including breakfast and dinner

Boesmanskop's swimming pool, abutting the vineyard. Opposite: The sitting room.

AZURA RETREAT

BENGUERRA ISLAND, MOZAMBIQUE

On a powdery stretch of tiny Benguerra Island, 14 miles from the mainland, this resort pulls out all the stops: private plunge pools and dedicated butlers; a head chef imported from England's Michelin three-starred Fat Duck. But as the first carbon-neutral property in Mozambique, the Azura is also eco-vigilant, with 15 thatch-fringed villas handmade from trees felled by past cyclones. Snorkel with the resident marine biologist, then visit the nearby school, one of the resort's gifts to the local community.

Benguerra Island, Mozambique; 27-11/258-0180; azura-retreats.com; doubles from $$$$$, all-inclusive, two-night minimum

Azura Retreat's beach villa with plunge pool.

A porch over-looking the Laikipia Plateau at Il Ngwesi Group Ranch & Lodge.

IL NGWESI GROUP RANCH & LODGE

LAIKIPIA PLATEAU, KENYA

A decade ago, these plains on the edge of the Great Rift Valley were dangerously overgrazed. But with help from an innovative trust, local Masai tribes switched from cattle herding to opening high-end lodges like Il Ngwesi. The 12-bed compound, solar-powered and made entirely of natural wood and grass, overlooks a 16,500-acre conservation area where elephants, lions, baboons, and giraffes abound. A day might begin with a safari before a lazy afternoon by the spring-fed infinity pool. For the sweetest dreams, book one of two rooms where you can pull your bed onto a platform and sleep under the stars.

Laikipia Plateau, Kenya; 25-46/431-405; ilngwesi.com; doubles from $$$$, all-inclusive

145

RELAIS DE LA REINE

ISALO, MADAGASCAR

Isalo National Park, in central Madagascar, is a moonscape of towering sandstone outcroppings, narrow canyons, and lush forest. Relais de la Reine, a collection of low-slung granite cottages, blends almost seamlessly into the surrounding area. The 37 rooms have polished wood floors, canopy beds, and private verandas. Saddle one of the property's Malagasy horses and ride to the nearby *piscine naturelle,* where swaying palms and thick vegetation shade a waterfall that spills into a deep, clear sandy-bottomed pool.

Ranohira, Isalo, Madagascar; 261-20/223-3623; doubles from $

An aerial view of Relais de la Reine.

A terrace in the main building at Tsara Komba Lodge.

TSARA KOMBA LODGE

NOSY KOMBA, MADAGASCAR

Tiny Nosy Komba has no roads, and therefore no cars; guests arrive from Nosy Be, the nearest island, a 25-minute boat ride away. Originally a three-bungalow getaway built by two solitude-loving Frenchmen, Tsara Komba now consists of eight private villas with a veranda-wrapped central hall, all overlooking the ocean. The spare interiors have four-poster beds and ceilings thatched with leaves from the local Ravenala tree. There are no TV's, Wi-Fi modems, or in-room telephones. Instead, cruise between coves in a pirogue, snorkel along a nearby reef, or visit a plantation of ylang-ylang, the jasmine-scented blossom used in Chanel No. 5.

Nosy Komba, Madagascar; 261-32/074-4040; tsarakomba.com; doubles from $$$

ANJAJAVY L'HÔTEL

MENABE SAKALAVA, MADAGASCAR

In the 1990's a French tycoon came to the island nation of Madagascar looking for a high-end place to stay, but couldn't find one, so he flew up the coast along the Mozambique Channel and discovered the perfect spot to build his own retreat. The 24 rosewood villas are scattered along a peninsula so remote that the resort was able to declare its own time zone—an hour ahead of the rest of the country—to capitalize on the luminous daylight. Two-story guest quarters have breakfast nooks, sitting rooms, and terraces with sea-facing hammocks. Afternoon tea is served on a large grassy knoll. Not to miss: an excursion to the *tsingy*, ancient limestone outcroppings jutting out of Moromba Bay.

Menabe Sakalava, Madagascar; 33-1/4469-1500; anjajavy.com; doubles from $$$$$, three-night minimum

Outdoor
seating at
Anjajavy
l'Hôtel's
restaurant.

RIAD MERIEM

MARRAKESH, MOROCCO

Riad hotels—traditional Moroccan houses with interior gardens—are popping up at a rapid clip in Marrakesh, so these days a property must truly be distinctive to stand out. Riad Meriem has had no problem turning heads. The five-room sanctuary, on one of the medina's oldest streets, is the creation of New York–based designer Thomas Hays, known for blending contemporary aesthetics with traditional techniques. His palette of muted aubergines and dusky pinks was inspired by natural Moroccan pigments. Antique African and Asian textiles punctuate the spare walls, and bathrooms have wash-basins crafted from Indian bronze pots. Dedicated to sourcing items locally as often as possible, Hays commissioned lamps and sconces from King Mohammed VI's own lamp maker: their tiny pinholes throw off speckled light patterns that turn the *riad* magical after dark.

97 Derb El Cadi, Azbezt, Marrakesh, Morocco; 212-24/387-731; riadmeriem.com; doubles from $, including breakfast

Riad Meriem's Aubergine room. Left: A hallway off the open-air veranda.

ANGSANA RIADS COLLECTION

MARRAKESH, MOROCCO

The first African venture of the Angsana hotel group—sister brand to Banyan Tree—is an inspired resort concept: seven converted private houses throughout Marrakesh. Riad Aida occupies a 19th-century frescoed former palace; Riad Bab Firdaus has a rooftop restaurant serving Moroccan and Thai food; Riad Lydines comes with a marble-chambered hammam, a library, and a lounge scattered with floor cushions—a perfect respite from the nonstop action of the medina.

Marrakesh, Morocco; 800/591-0439 or 65/6849-5788; angsana. com; doubles from $$

One of six bedrooms in Angsana's Riad Aida.

The Six Senses spa at Sharq Village.

SHARQ VILLAGE & SPA

DOHA, QATAR

Sheikh Hamad bin Khalifa al-Thani, the emir of Qatar, oversaw the construction of this 174-room property. Designed to evoke characteristic local dwellings and a marble royal palace, the resort comes complete with 1,050-count Frette linens and mosaic tiles of 18-karat gold. Handwoven kilims front carved-cedar beds, and courtyards are dotted with fountains—a symbol of wealth in this arid land. The attention to detail extends to the restaurant Al Liwan, where Middle Eastern dishes are made from sumac and halloumi cheese flown in from Lebanon.

Ras Abu Aboud St., Doha, Qatar; 800/241-3333 or 011-974/425-6666; sharqvillage.com; doubles from $$$

Jia Shanghai's
lobby, designed
by André Fu.

ASIA

BANYAN TREE LIJIANG

LIJIANG, CHINA

Lijiang, a UNESCO World Heritage Site known as "the Venice of Asia" for its centuries-old network of canals and bridges, sits in a forested nook of mountainous Yunnan province. The recently opened Banyan Tree resort is as picturesque as its location. Each of the 88 traditional curved-roof villas is set in its own walled garden; opulent red fabrics and lacquered furniture accent the polished interiors. Shining pools and ponds dot the property, reflecting Lijiang's intimate association with water.

Yuerong Rd., Shuhe, Lijiang, Yunnan, China; 800/591-0439 or 86-88/8533-1111; banyantree.com; doubles from $$, including breakfast

A villa with
a private pool
at Banyan
Tree Lijiang.

URBN HOTEL

SHANGHAI, CHINA

China isn't exactly known for sustainability, but the new Urbn Hotels & Resorts group aims to change that. The company's first property, a former factory and post office in central Shanghai, was built using floorboards and bricks salvaged from demolished buildings, and cools its 26 rooms with energy-efficient air conditioners and bamboo solar shades. Urbn does its part to offset its own carbon footprint by purchasing credits that fund ecological projects across China. The hotel also helps guests connect with the local culture: concierges can arrange for classes on Chinese cooking, acupuncture, and more.

183 Jiao Zhou Rd., Shanghai, China; 86-21/5153-4600; urbnhotels.com; doubles from $

roon

Restaurant &
Lounge

Roomtwentyeight
restaurant,
at Shanghai's
Urbn Hotel.
Opposite: Urbn's
room No. 6.

Jia Shanghai's lobby, with washed-oak flooring and sculptures by Chinese artists.

JIA SHANGHAI

SHANGHAI, CHINA

Ensconced in a 1920's building on fashionable West Nanjing Road, this 55-room hotel brings a much-needed dose of boutique intimacy to Shanghai's booming hotel scene. The eclectic Asian-contemporary interiors play richly embroidered fabrics and elegant birdcages off Minotti and Moroso furniture and cutting-edge sculpture. Jia means "home" in Mandarin, a fitting name given the host of amenities: well-stocked marble kitchenettes, in-room board games, and Wi-Fi—still a luxury among upscale properties here.

931 W. Nanjing Rd., Jingan, Shanghai, China; 86-21/6217-9000; jiashanghai.com; doubles from $$

Barolo, the
Ritz-Carlton's
Italian restaurant.

RITZ-CARLTON, BEIJING

BEIJING, CHINA

The Chaoyang District, with its high-end shops (Marc Jacobs, Ferragamo) is one of the most dynamic neighborhoods in a fast-paced town. This recently unveiled Ritz-Carlton joins its popular financial-district sibling, an Asian-inspired business hotel. In true Ritz-Carlton style, the property offers cosseting service and a sophisticated atmosphere. The lobby is decorated with carved wooden screens; the 27,000-square-foot spa has a heated lap pool and Balinese and Chinese therapists. The hotel also houses two trend-setting restaurants: Barolo, for Italian food, and Yu, which specializes in Cantonese dishes.

83A Jian Guo Rd., Chaoyang District, Beijing, China; 800/542-8680 or 86-10/5908-8888; ritzcarlton.com; doubles from $$$

PARK HYATT, BEIJING

BEIJING, CHINA

Soaring above the Central Business District like a beacon of Beijing's explosive growth, the new John Portman–designed mixed-use Yintai Centre is, at 820 feet tall, the city's loftiest development. The 237-room Park Hyatt occupies 19 floors of this new landmark address. Interiors, by Los Angeles's Remedios Simbieda, are spa-like and soothing. Freestanding limestone tubs, heated floors, streamlined furnishings, and a subdued palette create a cocooning effect. Topping it all, the hotel's 66th-floor restaurant, China Grill, serves updated Asian dishes (steamed abalone with black beans and chili, Wagyu sirloin)—amid 360-degree views.

2 Jianguomenwai St., Chaoyang District, Beijing, China; 800/233-1234 or 86-10/8567-1234; parkhyatt.com; doubles from $$

A guest room at the Park Hyatt.

LUXE MANOR

HONG KONG, CHINA

In a city slow to embrace the design hotel concept, eccentric Luxe Manor, in Kowloon's vibrant Tsim Sha Tsui district, is certainly making a statement. The 159-room Salvador Dalí–inspired hotel takes European opulence to maximalist heights. In some rooms, curvy Art Nouveau–style furniture sets off geometric-patterned carpets and bordello-red walls; faux family heirlooms and other flourishes skirt a fine line between surrealism and kitsch. The lobby's oversize, studded-leather poufs dot a floor covered in clock faces—in homage to the Surrealist master himself.

39 Kimberley Rd., Tsim Sha Tsui, Kowloon, Hong Kong, China; 852/3763-8888; theluxemanor.com; doubles from $$

Room no. 403 at Luxe Manor.

TAJ TASHI

THIMPHU, BHUTAN

The remote Himalayan kingdom of Bhutan has been slow to open to visitors. Thanks to the Taj hotel group, intrepid travelers now have an upscale lodging option right in the capital's heart. The design of the 66-room hotel evokes a *dzong*, or monastery-fort. Elements of traditional Bhutanese culture (handwoven carpets, nature-themed murals) are a fitting complement to the spectacular views of the mountains that surround the valley. Trek all day in the foothills, then curl up in the chic white-on-white lounge with a steaming cup of yak-butter tea.

Samten Lam, Thimphu, Bhutan; 866/969-1825 or 97-52/336-699; tajhotels.com; doubles from $$

A guest room at Taj Tashi, with a hand-painted cloud mural on the wall.

A canal-side villa at Kumarakom Lake Resort, left. Above right: One of the resort's houseboats, which can be rented by guests.

KUMARAKOM LAKE RESORT

KUMARAKOM, INDIA

Located between Vembanad Lake and a labyrinthine network of rivers, canals, streams, and lagoons that form Kerala's famed backwaters, Kumarakom Lake Resort is in one of the most idyllic parts of southwestern India. The 59 heritage villas have private Jacuzzis or pools, open-air showers, and views of migratory birds settling over the lake at sunset. The restaurant, housed in a 200-year-old octagonal mansion, serves seafood fresh from the coast—prawns cooked in coconut cream, fish wrapped in banana leaves. Rent one of the resort's thatched houseboats and lazily drift past cameos of village life.

Kumarakom, Kerala, India; 800/425-5030 or 91-48/1252-4900; klresort.com; doubles from $$, two-night minimum, including breakfast

The entrance to Samode Palace's main courtyard.

SAMODE PALACE

SAMODE, INDIA

Set in a sleepy hillside village in Rajasthan's Aravalli Range, Samode Palace is a perfect example of Rajput-Moghul architecture, with filigree-edged archways, a succession of courtyards, and frescoed walls. The 43 light-filled guest rooms feature elaborate marble work and woodwork; cotton dhurrie rugs cover mosaic-patterned floors. Ask the staff to show you around the intricately painted Darbar Hall and the magnificent Sheesh Mahal, or hall of mirrors.

Samode, District Jaipur, Rajasthan, India; 800/323-7500 or 91-1423/240-014; preferredhotels.com; doubles from $

UMAID BHAWAN PALACE

JODHPUR, INDIA

Commissioned in the 1930's, Umaid Bhawan fuses classic Rajasthani architecture (jutting towers) and period Western design (elegant friezes on a symmetrical façade). The maharajah of Jodhpur lives in one wing with his family; after a $15 million renovation by Taj Hotels, another portion is now open to guests. The Art Deco–inspired rooms feature curved flame-veneer headboards and scalloped-edge love seats. Peacocks roam 26 acres of gardens; there's a jewel box subterranean pool. At the center rises a 105-foot cupola that lets golden light through to the marble corridors below.

Circuit House Rd., Jodhpur, Rajasthan, India; 866/969-1825 or 91-291/251-0101; tajhotels.com; doubles from $$$$

The exterior of Umaid Bhawan Palace.

Rattan chairs and handblown-glass pendant lamps on Casa Colombo's veranda.

CASA COLOMBO

COLOMBO, SRI LANKA

This 200-year-old colonial mansion, on a peaceful cul-de-sac in the middle of bustling Colombo, has been converted into Sri Lanka's most glamorous new hotel. In each of the 12 suites, original details—floral-pattern mosaic floors, hand-carved ceilings, ornate balconies—are set off with such contemporary touches as freestanding copper tubs and waterfall showers. Curvy glass daybeds in the courtyard surround a pink-tiled pool. In the lounge, raw-silk–wrapped sofas front a polished cement wall. Hate to tear yourself away? The airport transfer in the hotel's vintage Austin is consolation.

231 Galle Rd., Bambalapitiya, Colombo, Sri Lanka; 94-11/452-0130; casacolombo. com; doubles from $

Seven's
Pink Room.

SEVEN

BANGKOK, THAILAND

Ten years ago, most Bangkok lodgings
were either big luxury hotels or grimy
backpacker dens. Things have changed,
thanks to a string of new small-scale
properties. Seven, one of the latest, occupies a town house on a quiet street in the
happening Sukhumvit neighborhood. A
collaboration between two Thai designers
and a cutting-edge London graphic arts
firm, the hotel's interiors include six guest
rooms individually decorated with murals
inspired by Buddhist philosophy. In
contrast, furnishings are clean and
spare—crisp white linens, angular tables
and chairs. The atmosphere is more like a
pied-à-terre than a hotel: guests receive cell
phones to use during their stay, plus a tip
sheet on the most buzzed-about bars and
restaurants in town.

3/15 Sukhumvit Soi 31, Bangkok, Thailand; 66-26/
620-951; sleepatseven.com; doubles from $

Guest rooms overlooking Alila Cha-am's nearly 500-foot-long reflecting pool.

ALILA CHA-AM

CHA-AM, THAILAND

Alila, in the emerging beach destination of Cha-Am, is a study in streamlined chic and wide-open oceanfront spaces. Designed by Duangrit Bunnag, a top Thai architect, the 79 rooms have soaring sandstone walls, platform featherbeds, floor-to-ceiling windows, and huge Dornbracht rain showers; villas each have a terrace with its own pool and garden. Let a hotel chef guide you through the area's markets or simply go shopping in the spa, which sells natural spritzes and scrubs locally made for the resort.

115 Moo 7, Bangkao, Petchaburi, Thailand; 66-32/709-555; alilahotels.com; doubles from $

171

A pool villa at Six Senses Hideaway Yao Noi.

SIX SENSES HIDEAWAY YAO NOI

PHANGNGA, THAILAND

This is the Asian seaside escape at its best: all the beauty of a remote destination without the hassle of being entirely off the grid. On the isle of Yao Noi, 45 minutes by boat from Phuket, guests are surrounded by lush jungle, tiny fishing villages, and untouched beaches. Perched on stilts, the 56 thatched-roof villas have private infinity pools, floor-to-ceiling windows, timber-paneled walls, and dedicated staff. Bamboo acts as a screen for the outdoor showers, and fridges are stocked with wines from around the world.

56 Moo 5, Koh Yao Noi, Phangnga, Thailand; 66-76/418-500; six-senses.com; doubles from $$$$$

The New Majestic's lobby, with the original concrete ceiling exposed.

NEW MAJESTIC

SINGAPORE

After owner Loh Lik Peng restored the New Majestic's 1928 Chinatown building, he turned over the interiors to local artists, filmmakers, and fashion designers. The result is dazzling: rooms clad in mirrors or eye-popping murals, furnished with hanging beds or glass-encased tubs. Peng's own eclectic antiques are scattered around the public spaces—vintage ceiling fans, dentist's chairs, signal lights from an old navy ship. The whimsy extends to the second-floor pool, lined with glassed portholes that give swimmers glimpses of the restaurant below.

31-37 Bukit Pasoh Rd., Singapore; 800/337-4685 or 65/6511-4700; designhotels.com; doubles from $

AMANKILA

BALI, INDONESIA

This slice of cliffside serenity on Bali's less developed east coast takes full advantage of its secluded location and Lombok Strait vistas. The 34 freestanding suites staggered on the jungle-clad slope have terraces hidden from view; many of them look onto the ocean. Rattan chaise longues, coconut-shell desks, and sunken bathtubs flecked with mother-of-pearl meld native influences with jet-set style. But the resort's showstopping feature is its extraordinary pool—three sapphire tiers inspired by the terraced rice paddies in the surrounding hills.

Manggis, Karangesam, Bali, Indonesia; 800/477-9180 or 62-363/41-333; amanresorts.com; doubles from $$$$

Amankila's three-tiered pool, overlooking the Lombok Strait.

175

Inside the
spa at Sentosa.
Opposite:
A villa pool.

SENTOSA

BALI, INDONESIA

Privacy and tranquillity prevail at Sentosa, an enclave of 38 villas with indoor-outdoor baths, individual pools and gardens, and fully stocked kitchen pavilions. The gym is a paean to wellness, offering nutritional advice as well as yoga and Pilates. And at Blossom, the resort's sexy restaurant-bar, expat Aussie Rob Sample puts a modern spin on traditional Indonesian food.

Jalan Pura Telaga Waja, Petitenget, Seminyak, Bali, Indonesia; 866/491-8372 or 62-361/730-333; balisentosa.com; villas from $$$

The lobby at
Hotel Tugu Bali.

HOTEL TUGU BALI

BALI, INDONESIA

This 21-room property in the beachfront village of Canggu is not just a hotel—it's an immersion in authentic Indonesian culture. Art collector Anhar Setjadibrata opened it to share his priceless antiques and introduce travelers to the island's traditions. Learn classical Balinese dance, study the gamelan, or accompany the chef to local markets, then take a cooking class. Finish with dinner in the rebuilt Chinese temple or on the lotus pavilion, and retire to a teak-floored room furnished with Dutch Colonial canopy beds, handwoven silks, and centuries-old sculptures.

Jalan Pantai Batu Bolong, Canggu, Bali, Indonesia; 800/225-4255 or 62-361/731-701; tuguhotels.com; doubles from $$

SPIDER HOUSE

BORACAY ISLAND, PHILIPPINES

Since its days as a rustic backpackers' haven—
where power was supplied by generators and ice
was ferried in—Boracay Island, 200 miles south of
Manila, has grown into a stylish tropical retreat.
Now resorts attract a global mix of travelers to
these powdery shores. Spider House is a Robinson
Crusoe fantasy of seven whitewashed, thatched-roof
bamboo bungalows, nestled in a jungly hill over the
turquoise sea. Rent an outrigger sailboat at nearby
White Beach to explore the island's coves, or wash
up on one of the hotel's ocean-facing verandas,
sip a San Miguel, and cultivate your inner castaway.

Diniwad Beach, Boracay Island, Philippines; 63-36/288-4568;
doubles from $

The cliffside
Spider House.

The Farm at
Cape Kidnappers,
on New Zealand's
North Island.

AUSTRALIA + NEW ZEALAND

Making up a
junior suite at the
Observatory Hotel.

OBSERVATORY HOTEL

SYDNEY, AUSTRALIA

Sydney's poshest old-school hotel is tucked in a residential pocket of the Rocks district—a discreet setting that draws an exclusive clientele. The 100 guest rooms are furnished with dark wood wardrobes and dressers, swagged drapes, and overstuffed chairs in brocade and chintz. One of the most impressive details is the subterranean pool: its vaulted ceiling twinkles like the night sky thanks to hundreds of fiber-optic "stars."

89-113 Kent St., Sydney, Australia; 800/237-1236 or 61-2/9256-2222; observatoryhotel.com.au; doubles from $$$

VOYAGES LIZARD ISLAND

GREAT BARRIER REEF, AUSTRALIA

WORLD'S BEST

With 24 beaches fringing the Great Barrier Reef, and accomodations for just 40 couples, Lizard Island is in a category all its own. Open-plan suites are done up in the blues and whites of the sea, with hammocks and decks discreetly hidden from view. Count on sunset cruises, torchlit beach dinners, and a staff that will do anything to please (including, once, hiding a diamond ring in a seashell to surprise a bride-to-be).

Lizard Island, Great Barrier Reef, Australia; 800/225-9849 or 61-2/8296-8010; lizardisland.com.au; doubles from $$$$$, all-inclusive, two-night minimum

A bungalow's private oceanfront daybed at Voyages Lizard Island.

PRAIRIE HOTEL

PARACHILNA, AUSTRALIA

The first thing that strikes you about Prairie Hotel is its isolation. Located in the remote former railway town of Parachilna, this outback lodge is a favorite of Aussies in the know. Eight spacious bedrooms are sunk in the ground up to the windows, protecting guests from the scalding summer heat. The rustic 1876 bar and dining room turn out classic country cooking, like rabbit-and-bacon potpie. The espresso is as good as any you'll find in Sydney; the Fargher lager, named for the owners and brewed only for the hotel, is even better.

High St., Parachilna, Australia; 61-8/8648-4844; prairiehotel.com.au; doubles from $

The restaurant at the Prairie Hotel, Jane and Ross Fargher's restored roadhouse.

ARKABA STATION

WILPENA POUND, AUSTRALIA

After purchasing Arkaba Station in 1984, Dean and Lizzie Rasheed spent two decades turning a portion of this working 19th-century sheep farm into a welcoming bush-country retreat. Two rooms in the original 1850's homestead now accommodate overnight guests, and two outbuildings have been converted into cottages with private verandas and expansive outback views. Join a four-wheel-drive excursion into the surrounding hills for kangaroo sightings and late-afternoon cocktails on a ridge overlooking the arid plain.

Off Hwy. 47, between Hawker and Wilpena Pound, Australia; 61-8/8648-4195; arkabastation.com; doubles from $

The outdoor dining area at Arkaba Station.

NORTH BUNDALEER HOMESTEAD

JAMESTOWN, AUSTRALIA

This 1901 house once anchored a single 23,000-acre farm; by the 1970's the pastureland had been subdivided and the house abandoned. But in 2002 the Victorian spread was rescued and converted into an inn. A herculean restoration uncovered William Morris wallpapers, original stained-glass windows, and traces of an elaborate drawing-room frieze, which a painter was hired to re-create. Rooms were updated with mahogany furniture, Chinese screens, and vases of flowers fresh from the garden. The meals are a similar mix of tradition and inspiration—roast beef comes with suet pudding and bordelaise sauce, rhubarb tart is made with mille-feuille—and are accompanied by wines from the nearby Clare Valley.

R. M. Williams Way, Jamestown, Australia; 61-8/8665-4024; northbundaleer.com.au; doubles from $$, including meals

The fully restored 1901 farmhouse at North Bundaleer Homestead.

SOUTHERN OCEAN LODGE

KANGAROO ISLAND, AUSTRALIA

On a sparsely populated island 30 minutes by plane from Adelaide sits this lodge, which is contemporary in design and green in attitude. The 21 spacious suites have limestone floors, artwork by local artisans, and outdoor terraces. Air-conditioning is unnecessary: the property was constructed to take advantage of natural weather patterns. Owners James and Hayley Baillie developed only one percent of their total acreage on the wildlife-filled isle, leaving the rest of the land in a preservation trust. Guests learn about the resort's sustainability policy upon check-in, underscoring the Baillies' appreciation of the landscape's natural beauty.

Hanson Bay, Kangaroo Island, Australia; 61-2/9918-4355; southernoceanlodge.com.au; doubles from $$$$$, all-inclusive, two-night minimum

The dining room
at Southern
Ocean Lodge.
Left: Terraces
maximize indoor-
outdoor living.

DIAMANT HOTEL

CANBERRA, AUSTRALIA

As Australia's capital, Canberra has plenty of clout, but it has never been known for style. The recently opened Diamant adds much-needed panache to the town's formerly fusty accommodation options. Its Art Deco shell has been dressed up with contemporary panes of glass and zinc; the 80 rooms are quirky and eclectic—riotous wallpaper on the ceilings, mother-of-pearl bathroom tiles—and include 21st-century amenities, like Bang & Olufsen plasma TV's. In the Parlour Wine Room, you can mingle with the local power brokers who are making this scene their own.

15 Edinburgh Ave., Canberra, Australia; 61-2/6175-2222; diamant.com.au; doubles from $

The Diamant
Hotel's lobby.
Opposite:
The dining
area of a suite.

Voyages Cradle Mountain Lodge's spa. Opposite: One of 20 planked walkways.

VOYAGES CRADLE MOUNTAIN LODGE

TASMANIA, AUSTRALIA

WORLD'S BEST An alpine wilderness retreat, Voyages Cradle Mountain Lodge has 86 timber cabins surrounded by ancient pines and crystalline lakes at the edge of one of the few remaining rain forests in the world. The spa specializes in holistic natural treatments, such as fennel-and–birch bark peels. But the real draw is the surrounding parkland, where explorations down the rambling boardwalk paths can lead to encounters with wombats, wallabies, and, yes, Tasmanian devils.

4038 Cradle Mountain Rd., Cradle Mountain, Tasmania, Australia; 61-3/6492-2100; cradlemountainlodge.com.au; doubles from $

The lounge at
the Farm at Cape
Kidnappers.
Opposite: The
lodge's stone-and-
wood exterior.

194

FARM AT CAPE KIDNAPPERS

HAWKE'S BAY, NEW ZEALAND

Set on a working ranch with views of the Pacific Ocean, this 26-room lodge uses natural fabrics, woods, and metals in sophisticated ways. Interior barn doors roll back to reveal marble-clad bathrooms and overstuffed leather chairs with shearling pillows; burlap curtains frame enormous windows that overlook paddocks and hills. Moody black-and-white sheep photographs and tractor seats hung like fine art put a cheeky spin on farm life. Settle in next to the dining room fireplace for roast lamb raised on-property. Now that's farm to table.

446 Clifton Rd., Te Awanga, Hawke's Bay, New Zealand; 64-6/875-1900; capekidnappers.com; doubles from $$$, all-inclusive

Treetops Lodge, surrounded by native hardwood forest.

TREETOPS LODGE & WILDERNESS EXPERIENCE

ROTORUA, NEW ZEALAND

WORLD'S BEST

This resort, located on New Zealand's North Island, believes that luxury and ecology can mix. Guests enter by a timber walkway that crosses a spring-fed brook filled with rainbow trout. The brook winds through the grounds and even flows beneath the lodge itself. Buildings are constructed of local stone and fallen trees milled on-site; the lobby's rimu-wood beams are carved with illustrations from Maori folklore. Room details include cast brass door pulls, copper light fixtures, fieldstone fireplaces, and well-broken-in leather sofas. There are many ways to explore the 2,500-acre estate: riding horseback through virgin rain forest, mountain biking miles of private trails, or fishing in the four lakes and seven streams.

351 Kearoa Rd., Rotorua, New Zealand; 64-7/333-2066; treetops.co.nz; villas from $$, all-inclusive

MATAKAURI LODGE & SPA

QUEENSTOWN, NEW ZEALAND

Queenstown runs on adrenaline: the birthplace of bungee jumping also offers skydiving, jet boating, and killer downhill slopes. Matakauri Lodge & Spa is just an eight-minute drive from the action, but feels a world away, set among cabbage trees and Douglas firs. The main lodge houses four suites; six villas dot the grounds. All have simple, stylish schist-and-wood interiors and views of Lake Wakatipu. At the just-opened spa, finish a day of heart-pounding adventure with a body wrap made from natural ingredients like kiwifruit and manuka honey, or go for a soak in the cedar Japanese-style hot tub.

Farrycroft Row, Rapid #571, Glenorchy Rd., Queenstown, New Zealand; 64-3/441-1008; matakauri.co.nz; doubles from $$$$, including breakfast and dinner

Matakauri Lodge & Spa, overlooking Lake Wakatipu and Cecil Peak.

197

T+L
WORLD'S
BEST
AWARDS

IN *TRAVEL + LEISURE*'S ANNUAL WORLD'S BEST AWARDS SURVEY, READERS
ARE ASKED TO RATE THEIR FAVORITE HOTELS AND SPAS AROUND THE
GLOBE, BASED ON LOCATION, FOOD, WINE, SERVICE, AND VALUE, AMONG
OTHER CRITERIA. EACH YEAR, THE CHANGING LIST OF WINNERS REVEALS
READERS' EVOLVING, BUT ALWAYS EXACTING, STANDARDS OF EXCELLENCE.
YOU'LL FIND THE MOST RECENT RESULTS ON THE FOLLOWING PAGES,
ORGANIZED BY REGION AND SCORED ON A SCALE OF 0 TO 100.

No. 1
SINGITA SABI SAND &
KRUGER NATIONAL PARK,
SOUTH AFRICA

WORLD'S BEST

WORLDWIDE

TOP 100 HOTELS

1 **Singita Sabi Sand & Kruger National Park** South Africa 97.50

2 **Oberoi Rajvilas** Jaipur, India 95.71

3 **Fairmont Mara Safari Club** Masai Mara, Kenya 95.58

4 **Oberoi Udaivilas** Udaipur, India 95.00

4 **Triple Creek Ranch** Darby, Montana 95.00

6 **Oberoi Amarvilas** Agra, India 94.27

7 **Kirawira Luxury Tented Camp** Serengeti National Park, Tanzania 93.89

8 **Sabi Sabi Private Game Reserve** Sabi Sands, South Africa 93.48

9 **Tortilis Camp** Amboseli National Park, Kenya 93.06

10 **Domaine des Hauts de Loire** Onzain, France 92.56

11 **Alvear Palace Hotel** Buenos Aires 92.44

12 **Little Palm Island Resort & Spa** Little Torch Key, Florida 92.39

13 **Hotel Bel-Air** Los Angeles 92.32

14 **Mandarin Oriental** Bangkok 91.94

15 **Four Seasons Resort Lanai, the Lodge at Koele** 91.88

16 **Kichwa Tembo** Masai Mara, Kenya 91.59

17 **Peninsula Bangkok** 91.51

18 **Taj Lake Palace** Udaipur, India 91.43

19 **Four Seasons Resort** Chiang Mai, Thailand 91.25

20 **Peninsula Beverly Hills** 91.15

21 **Hotel Hassler** Rome 91.10

22 **Cape Grace** Cape Town 91.05

23 **Peninsula Hong Kong** 91.04

24 **Voyages Lizard Island** Australia 90.94

25 **Treetops Lodge & Wilderness Experience** Rotorua, New Zealand 90.77

26 **Four Seasons Resort Maui at Wailea** 90.64

27 **Four Seasons Resort Hualalai** Hawaii 90.63

27 **Wickaninnish Inn** Tofino, Vancouver Island 90.63

29 **Four Seasons Hotel** Hong Kong 90.37

30 **Hotel Amigo** Brussels 90.20

31 **Hotel Monasterio** Cuzco, Peru 90.16

32 **Il San Pietro** Positano, Italy 90.13

33 **Four Seasons Hotel George V** Paris 90.08

34 **Four Seasons Hotel Gresham Palace** Budapest 90.00

35 **Four Seasons Hotel** New York City 89.94

36 **Peninsula Beijing** 89.92

37 **Auberge du Soleil** Rutherford, California 89.89

38 **Four Seasons Hotel México D.F.** Mexico City 89.82

39 **Mount Kenya Safari Club** Nanyuki, Kenya 89.71

40 **Post Ranch Inn** Big Sur, California 89.65

41 **Four Seasons Hotel Istanbul at Sultanahmet** 89.57

42 **Montage Laguna Beach** California 89.55

43 **Four Seasons Hotel** Prague 89.47

44 **Halekulani** Honolulu 89.45

45 **Peninsula Chicago** 89.38

46 **Four Seasons Resort** Jackson Hole, Wyoming 89.36

47 **Grace in Rosebank** Johannesburg 89.32

48 **One & Only Ocean Club** Paradise Island, Bahamas 89.29

49 **Bernardus Lodge** Carmel Valley, California 89.27

50 **Four Seasons Hotel** Chicago 89.24

51 **San Clemente Palace Hotel & Resort** Venice 89.17

52 **Raffles Hotel** Singapore 89.03

53 **Grand Hotel Baglioni** Bologna, Italy 89.00

54 **Beverly Hills Hotel & Bungalows** 88.99

55 **Four Seasons Resort Whistler** British Columbia 88.94

56 **Four Seasons Resort, The Biltmore** Santa Barbara, California 88.82

57 **Le Méridien Bristol** Warsaw 88.81

58 **Ritz-Carlton, Bachelor Gulch** Beaver Creek, Colorado 88.78

59 **La Casa Que Canta** Zihuatanejo, Mexico 88.75

60 **St. Regis Hotel** Shanghai 88.70

61 **Ngorongoro Crater Lodge** Tanzania 88.67

62 **Victoria-Jungfrau Grand Hotel & Spa** Interlaken, Switzerland 88.65

63 **Inn at Little Washington** Washington, Virginia 88.58

64 **Four Seasons Hotel** Shanghai 88.51

65 **Hotel Goldener Hirsch** Salzburg 88.50

65 **Tides Zihuatanejo** Mexico 88.50

67 **Çiragan Palace Kempinski** Istanbul 88.41

68 **Hotel Hana-Maui & Honua Spa** Maui 88.40

69 **Villa d'Este** Cernobbio, Italy 88.39

70 **Stein Eriksen Lodge** Park City, Utah 88.38

71 **Ritz-Carlton, Laguna Niguel** California 88.35

72 **Portman Ritz-Carlton** Shanghai 88.28

|||||||||||||||||||||||||||||||||||||||||||||||||||||||||||||||||||||||||||||||||||||||||||||||

Throughout the World's Best Awards, scores are rounded to the nearest hundredth of a point; in the event of a tie, properties share the same ranking.

No. 92
CALISTOGA RANCH,
CALIFORNIA

TOP 20 HOTEL SPAS

No. 2
WORLDWIDE SPA
FOUR SEASONS RESORT,
CHIANG MAI, THAILAND

No. 17
RITZ-CARLTON,
BACHELOR GULCH,
BEAVER CREEK, COLORADO

TOP 100 HOTELS

1   **Triple Creek Ranch** Darby, Montana 95.00
2   **Little Palm Island Resort & Spa** Little Torch Key, Florida 92.39
3   **Hotel Bel-Air** Los Angeles 92.32
4   **Peninsula Beverly Hills** 91.15
5   **Wickaninnish Inn** Tofino, Vancouver Island 90.63
6   **Four Seasons Hotel** New York City 89.94
7   **Auberge du Soleil** Rutherford, California 89.89
8   **Post Ranch Inn** Big Sur, California 89.65
9   **Montage Laguna Beach** California 89.55
10 **Peninsula Chicago** 89.38
11 **Four Seasons Resort** Jackson Hole, Wyoming 89.36
12 **Bernardus Lodge** Carmel Valley, California 89.27
13 **Four Seasons Hotel** Chicago 89.24
14 **Beverly Hills Hotel & Bungalows** 88.99
15 **Four Seasons Resort Whistler** British Columbia 88.94
16 **Four Seasons Resort The Biltmore** Santa Barbara, California 88.82
17 **Ritz-Carlton, Bachelor Gulch** Beaver Creek, Colorado 88.78
18 **Inn at Little Washington** Washington, Virginia 88.58
19 **Stein Eriksen Lodge** Park City, Utah 88.38
20 **Ritz-Carlton, Laguna Niguel** California 88.35
21 **Post Hotel & Spa** Lake Louise, Alberta 88.26
22 **Little Nell** Aspen, Colorado 88.23
23 **Royal Palms Resort & Spa** Phoenix 88.15
24 **Hotel Healdsburg** California 87.77
25 **Auberge Saint-Antoine** Quebec City 87.72
26 **Calistoga Ranch** California 87.58
27 **Rusty Parrot Lodge & Spa** Jackson Hole, Wyoming 87.50
28 **The Cloister at Sea Island** Georgia 87.38
29 **The James** Chicago 86.84
30 **Rittenhouse Hotel** Philadelphia 86.59
31 **Charleston Place** South Carolina 86.51
32 **Lodge at Pebble Beach** California 86.48
32 **Ritz-Carlton New York, Central Park** 86.48
34 **Four Seasons Hotel** Las Vegas 86.46
35 **Balsams Grand Resort Hotel** Dixville Notch, New Hampshire 86.36
36 **Inn on Biltmore Estate** Asheville, North Carolina 86.32
37 **Metropolitan Hotel Vancouver** 86.08
38 **Four Seasons Hotel** San Francisco 86.07

39 **Ritz-Carlton** Naples, Florida 85.93
40 **Blackberry Farm** Walland, Tennessee 85.89
41 **Windsor Court Hotel** New Orleans 85.76
42 **Rimrock Resort Hotel** Banff, Alberta 85.74
43 **Ventana Inn & Spa** Big Sur, California 85.69
44 **Inn at the Market** Seattle 85.60
45 **Langham Huntington Hotel & Spa (formerly Ritz-Carlton Huntington Hotel & Spa)** Pasadena, California 85.59
46 **Four Seasons Resort** Palm Beach, Florida 85.58
47 **Inn at Spanish Bay** Pebble Beach, California 85.57
48 **Bellagio** Las Vegas 85.54
49 **Lodge at Torrey Pines** La Jolla, California 85.51
50 **Ritz-Carlton, Georgetown** Washington, D.C. 85.49
51 **XV Beacon** Boston 85.46
52 **Mirror Lake Inn Resort & Spa** Lake Placid, New York 85.44
53 **Four Seasons Resort Aviara** North San Diego 85.42
54 **Four Seasons Resort & Club Dallas at Las Colinas** 85.39
54 **Park Hyatt Beaver Creek Resort & Spa** Colorado 85.39
56 **Ritz-Carlton** Chicago 85.28
57 **Planters Inn** Charleston, South Carolina 85.26
58 **Four Seasons Hotel** Boston 85.23
59 **Enchantment Resort** Sedona, Arizona 85.22
60 **Ritz-Carlton Lodge, Reynolds Plantation** Greensboro, Georgia 85.11
61 **The Hay-Adams** Washington, D.C. 85.04
62 **Ponte Vedra Inn & Club** Florida 85.03
62 **Ritz-Carlton** San Francisco 85.03
62 **Mandarin Oriental** New York City 85.03
65 **The Breakers** Palm Beach, Florida 84.94
66 **Four Seasons Hotel** Vancouver 84.85
67 **Four Seasons Hotel** Philadelphia 84.81
68 **Watercolor Inn & Resort** Santa Rosa Beach, Florida 84.75
69 **Lake Placid Lodge** New York 84.71
70 **The Greenbrier** White Sulphur Springs, West Virginia 84.69
71 **Fairmont Chateau Lake Louise** Alberta 84.62
72 **St. Regis Resort Monarch Beach** California 84.61
73 **Eliot Hotel** Boston 84.57
74 **Prince of Wales Hotel** Niagara-on-the-Lake, Ontario 84.52
75 **The Phoenician, A Luxury Collection Resort** Scottsdale, Arizona 84.41
76 **Sanctuary at Kiawah Island Golf Resort** South Carolina 84.36
77 **Fairmont Vancouver Airport** 84.24

No. 81
WYNN LAS VEGAS

TOP 25 HOTEL SPAS

TOP 10 DESTINATION SPAS

HAWAII

TOP 25 HOTELS

No. 7
FOUR SEASONS
RESORT LANAI
AT MANELE BAY

CARIBBEAN + THE BAHAMAS + BERMUDA

TOP 25 HOTELS

1. **One & Only Ocean Club** Paradise Island, Bahamas 89.29
2. **Four Seasons Resort** Nevis 88.05
3. **The Reefs** Bermuda 87.08
4. **CuisinArt Resort & Spa** Anguilla 87.07
5. **Couples Swept Away** Negril, Jamaica 85.45
6. **Rosewood Little Dix Bay** Virgin Gorda, British Virgin Islands 85.44
7. **Ritz-Carlton** Grand Cayman, Cayman Islands 85.23
8. **Couples Negril** Jamaica 85.17
9. **Parrot Cay** Turks and Caicos 84.55
10. **Cap Juluca** Anguilla 84.48
11. **Peter Island Resort** British Virgin Islands 83.85
12. **Caneel Bay, A Rosewood Resort** St. John, U.S. Virgin Islands 82.96
13. **Half Moon** Rose Hall, Jamaica 82.86
14. **Ritz-Carlton** St. Thomas, U.S. Virgin Islands 82.35
15. **The Buccaneer** St. Croix, U.S. Virgin Islands 81.96
16. **Casa de Campo** La Romana, Dominican Republic 81.38
17. **Ritz-Carlton, San Juan Hotel, Spa & Casino** Puerto Rico 80.65
18. **Elbow Beach** Bermuda 79.88
19. **Radisson Aruba Resort, Casino & Spa** 79.55
20. **Hotel el Convento** San Juan, Puerto Rico 79.36
21. **Hyatt Regency Aruba Resort & Casino** 78.02
22. **Sandals Grande St. Lucian Spa & Beach Resort** St. Lucia 77.97
23. **Sandals Whitehouse European Village & Spa** Westmoreland, Jamaica 77.50
24. **Grand Lido Negril Resort & Spa** Jamaica 77.39
25. **Sandals Grande Antigua Resort & Spa** 77.14

No. 1
FOUR SEASONS RESORT, NEVIS

TOP 10 HOTEL SPAS

1. **Four Seasons Resort** Nevis 90.88
2. **Ritz-Carlton** Grand Cayman, Cayman Islands 90.10
3. **One & Only Ocean Club** Paradise Island, Bahamas 89.47
4. **Ritz-Carlton, San Juan Hotel, Spa & Casino** Puerto Rico 84.72
5. **Couples Swept Away** Westmoreland, Jamaica 83.33
6. **Ritz-Carlton** St. Thomas, U.S. Virgin Islands 83.13
7. **Rosewood Little Dix Bay** Virgin Gorda, British Virgin Islands 82.99
8. **Fairmont Southampton** Bermuda 82.81
9. **Four Seasons Resort Great Exuma at Emerald Bay** Bahamas 82.59
10. **Punta Cana Resort & Club** Dominican Republic 82.50

No. 18
LLAO LLAO HOTEL & RESORT
GOLF SPA, SAN CARLOS
DE BARILOCHE, ARGENTINA

MEXICO + CENTRAL + SOUTH AMERICA

TOP 25 HOTELS

1   **Alvear Palace Hotel** Buenos Aires 92.44
2   **Hotel Monasterio** Cuzco, Peru 90.16
3   **Four Seasons Hotel México D.F.** Mexico City 89.82
4   **La Casa Que Canta** Zihuatanejo, Mexico 88.75
5   **Tides Zihuatanejo** Mexico 88.50
6   **Occidental Royal Hideaway Playacar** Playa del Carmen, Mexico 88.04
7   **Le Méridien Cancún Resort & Spa** 87.84
8   **Four Seasons Hotel** Buenos Aires 87.66
9   **Hotel Punta Islita** Guanacaste, Costa Rica 87.50
10 **Inkaterra Machu Picchu Hotel** Peru 87.24
11 **Ritz-Carlton** Santiago, Chile 87.16
12 **Las Ventanas al Paraíso, A Rosewood Resort** Los Cabos, Mexico 86.84
13 **One & Only Palmilla** Los Cabos, Mexico 86.69
14 **Park Hyatt** Mendoza, Argentina 86.01
15 **Miraflores Park Hotel** Lima, Peru 85.85
16 **JW Marriott Hotel** Lima, Peru 85.77
17 **Ritz-Carlton** Cancún 85.61
18 **Llao Llao Hotel & Resort Golf Spa** San Carlos de Bariloche, Argentina 85.60
19 **Tides Riviera Maya** Playa del Carmen, Mexico 85.50
20 **Esperanza Resort** Los Cabos, Mexico 85.11
21 **Four Seasons Resort Costa Rica at Peninsula Papagayo** 85.00
22 **Four Seasons Resort Punta Mita** Mexico 84.90
23 **Grand Hyatt** Santiago, Chile 84.86
24 **Bristol Hotel** Panama City, Panama 84.76
25 **Fairmont Acapulco Princess** Mexico 83.86

No. 4
LA CASA QUE CANTA,
ZIHUATANEJO, MEXICO

TOP 10 HOTEL SPAS

1   **Maroma Resort & Spa** Solidaridad, Mexico 90.79
2   **Esperanza** Los Cabos, Mexico 90.63
3   **Las Ventanas al Paraíso, A Rosewood Resort** Los Cabos, Mexico 86.96
4   **JW Marriott Cancún Resort & Spa** 86.49
5   **Four Seasons Resort Costa Rica at Peninsula Papagayo** 85.94
6   **One & Only Palmilla** Los Cabos, Mexico 84.66
7   **Four Seasons Resort Punta Mita** Mexico 84.56
8   **Dreams Cancún Resort & Spa** 84.03
9   **Ritz-Carlton** Cancún 83.64
10 **Tides Zihuatanejo** Mexico 83.50

WORLD'S BEST

EUROPE

TOP 50 HOTELS

1   **Domaine des Hauts de Loire** Onzain, France 92.56
2   **Hotel Hassler** Rome 91.10
3   **Hotel Amigo** Brussels 90.20
4   **Il San Pietro** Positano, Italy 90.13
5   **Four Seasons Hotel George V** Paris 90.08
6   **Four Seasons Hotel Gresham Palace** Budapest 90.00
7   **Four Seasons Hotel Istanbul at Sultanahmet** 89.57
8   **Four Seasons Hotel** Prague 89.47
9   **San Clemente Palace Hotel & Resort** Venice 89.17
10 **Grand Hotel Baglioni** Bologna, Italy 89.00
11 **Le Méridien Bristol** Warsaw 88.81
12 **Victoria-Jungfrau Grand Hotel & Spa** Interlaken, Switzerland 88.65

13 **Hotel Goldener Hirsch** Salzburg 88.50
14 **Çiragan Palace Kempinski** Istanbul 88.41
15 **Villa d'Este** Cernobbio, Italy 88.39
16 **Hotel Bristol** Vienna 87.93
17 **The Dorchester** London 87.88
18 **Ritz Paris** 87.86
19 **Grand Hotel Quisisana** Capri, Italy 87.67
20 **Baur au Lac** Zürich 87.63
21 **Le Sirenuse** Positano, Italy 87.60
22 **Palazzo Sasso** Ravello, Italy 86.84
23 **Château Les Crayères** Reims, France 86.82
24 **Bauer Il Palazzo** Venice 86.63
25 **The Balmoral** Edinburgh 86.60
26 **Swissôtel The Bosphorus** Istanbul 86.36
27 **Capri Palace Hotel & Spa** Italy 86.29
28 **Park Hyatt Paris-Vendôme** 86.23
29 **Grande Bretagne, A Luxury Collection Hotel** Athens 86.10
30 **Four Seasons Hotel** Milan 85.75
31 **Kempinski Hotel Corvinus** Budapest 85.71
32 **Four Seasons Hotel** Dublin 85.68
33 **Merrion Hotel** Dublin 85.62
34 **Park Hotel Kenmare** County Kerry, Ireland 85.50
35 **Grand Hotel Villa Medici** Florence 85.43
36 **Mandarin Oriental Hyde Park** London 85.40
37 **Adare Manor Hotel & Golf Resort** County Limerick, Ireland 85.21
38 **Dromoland Castle** County Clare, Ireland 85.06
39 **Waterford Castle Hotel & Golf Club** Ireland 84.75
39 **Hôtel de Paris** Monaco 84.75
41 **Claridge's** London 84.56
42 **Grand Hôtel** Stockholm 84.55
43 **Westin Palace** Madrid 84.07
44 **Gritti Palace, A Luxury Collection Hotel** Venice 83.99
45 **Grand Hotel Miramare** Santa Margherita Ligure, Italy 83.97
46 **King George Palace** Athens 83.89
47 **Bauer Hotel** Venice 83.79
48 **St. Regis Grand** Rome 83.55
49 **Westin Excelsior** Florence 83.54
50 **Ashford Castle** County Mayo, Ireland 83.53

No. 21
LE SIRENUSE,
POSITANO, ITALY

No. 4
SABI SABI PRIVATE GAME
RESERVE, SABI SANDS,
SOUTH AFRICA

WORLD'S
BEST

AFRICA + THE MIDDLE EAST

TOP 25 HOTELS

1 **Singita Sabi Sand & Kruger National Park** South Africa 97.50
2 **Fairmont Mara Safari Club** Masai Mara, Kenya 95.58
3 **Kirawira Luxury Tented Camp** Serengeti National Park, Tanzania 93.89
4 **Sabi Sabi Private Game Reserve** Sabi Sands, South Africa 93.48
5 **Tortilis Camp** Amboseli National Park, Kenya 93.06
6 **Kichwa Tembo** Masai Mara, Kenya 91.59
7 **Cape Grace** Cape Town 91.05
8 **Mount Kenya Safari Club** Nanyuki, Kenya 89.71
9 **Grace in Rosebank** Johannesburg 89.32
10 **Ngorongoro Crater Lodge** Tanzania 88.67
11 **The Westcliff** Johannesburg 87.67
12 **Ngorongoro Sopa Lodge** Tanzania 86.96
13 **Fairmont the Norfolk Hotel** Nairobi 86.87
14 **Royal Livingstone** Zambia 85.74
15 **Serengeti Sopa Lodge** Tanzania 85.28
16 **Mount Nelson Hotel** Cape Town 85.00
17 **Mena House Oberoi** Cairo 82.89
18 **King David Hotel** Jerusalem 82.86
19 **Ngorongoro Serena Safari Lodge** Tanzania 82.50
19 **Sweetwaters Tented Camp** Ol Pejeta Conservancy, Kenya 82.50
21 **Serengeti Serena Safari Lodge** Tanzania 81.68
22 **Amboseli Serena Safari Lodge** Kenya 81.09
23 **Lake Manyara Serena Safari Lodge** Tanzania 81.00
24 **Victoria Falls Hotel** Zimbabwe 80.00
25 **JW Marriott Hotel** Cairo 79.36

No. 16
MOUNT NELSON HOTEL,
CAPE TOWN

WORLD'S
BEST

ASIA

TOP 50 HOTELS

1 **Oberoi Rajvilas** Jaipur, India 95.71
2 **Oberoi Udaivilas** Udaipur, India 95.00
3 **Oberoi Amarvilas** Agra, India 94.27
4 **Mandarin Oriental** Bangkok 91.94
5 **Peninsula Bangkok** 91.51
6 **Taj Lake Palace** Udaipur, India 91.43
7 **Four Seasons Resort** Chiang Mai, Thailand 91.25
8 **Peninsula Hong Kong** 91.04
9 **Four Seasons Hotel** Hong Kong 90.37

10 **Peninsula Beijing** 89.92
11 **Raffles Hotel** Singapore 89.03
12 **St. Regis Hotel** Shanghai 88.70
13 **Four Seasons Hotel** Shanghai 88.51
14 **Portman Ritz-Carlton** Shanghai 88.28
15 **Raffles Grand Hotel d'Angkor** Siem Reap, Cambodia 88.16
16 **Park Hyatt** Tokyo 88.09
17 **InterContinental** Hong Kong 87.57
18 **St. Regis Hotel** Beijing 87.08
19 **Shangri-La Hotel** Bangkok 86.88
20 **Ritz-Carlton Millenia** Singapore 86.66
21 **Taj Mahal Palace & Tower** Mumbai, India 86.34
22 **Imperial Hotel** Tokyo 86.24
23 **Mandarin Oriental** Singapore 86.21
24 **Westin Bund Center** Shanghai 86.09
25 **Grand Hyatt** Taipei 86.02
26 **JW Marriott Phuket Resort & Spa** Thailand 86.00
27 **Rambagh Palace** Jaipur, India 85.98
28 **Fairmont (formerly Raffles the Plaza)** Singapore 85.36
29 **La Résidence Phou Vao** Luang Prabang, Laos 85.24
30 **Mandarin Oriental** Hong Kong 85.17
31 **Kowloon Shangri-La** Hong Kong 85.14
32 **Park Hyatt Saigon** Ho Chi Minh City, Vietnam 85.00
33 **The Oberoi** New Delhi 84.80
34 **Pudong Shangri-La** Shanghai 84.78
35 **Grand Hyatt** Shanghai 84.46
36 **Royal Orchid Sheraton Hotel & Towers** Bangkok 84.41
37 **Conrad** Hong Kong 83.77
38 **Taj Mahal Hotel** New Delhi 83.42
39 **JW Marriott Hotel** Bangkok 82.57
39 **JW Marriott Hotel Shanghai at Tomorrow Square** 82.57
41 **Sheraton Grande Sukhumvit** Bangkok 82.50
42 **Grand Hyatt** Singapore 82.36
43 **Sofitel Metropole** Hanoi 81.94
44 **JW Marriott Hotel** Hong Kong 81.74
45 **Grand Hyatt** Hong Kong 80.88
46 **Raffles Hotel Le Royal** Phnom Penh, Cambodia 80.81
47 **Grand Hyatt** Beijing 80.68
48 **Shangri-La Hotel** Beijing 80.64
49 **China World Hotel** Beijing 80.43
50 **The Imperial** New Delhi 80.22

No. 5
PENINSULA
BANGKOK

No. 30
MANDARIN ORIENTAL,
HONG KONG

WORLD'S
BEST

AUSTRALIA + NEW ZEALAND + THE SOUTH PACIFIC

TOP 25 HOTELS

1   **Voyages Lizard Island** Australia 90.94
2   **Treetops Lodge & Wilderness Experience** Rotorua, New Zealand 90.77
3   **Westin Sydney Hotel** 87.50
4   **Huka Lodge** Taupo, New Zealand 87.00
5   **Four Seasons Hotel** Sydney 86.24
6   **Park Hyatt** Sydney 85.47
7   **Grand Hyatt** Melbourne 85.12
8   **Park Hyatt** Melbourne 83.73
9   **The Langham** Melbourne 82.21
10 **Sebel Reef House & Spa** Palm Cove, Australia 81.54
11 **Hyatt Regency** Auckland 81.30
12 **Millbrook Resort** Queenstown, New Zealand 81.25
13 **The George** Christchurch, New Zealand 80.78
14 **InterContinental** Sydney 80.70
15 **Sofitel** Melbourne 79.55
16 **Voyages Cradle Mountain Lodge** Tasmania 79.17
17 **Sheraton on the Park** Sydney 78.70
18 **Hayman** Great Barrier Reef, Australia 78.57
19 **InterContinental Resort & Spa** Moorea, French Polynesia 78.00
20 **Hilton** Auckland 77.52
21 **Voyages Longitude 131°** Ayers Rock, Australia 77.12
22 **Kewarra Beach Resort** Australia 76.46
23 **Lilianfels Blue Mountains Resort & Spa** Australia 75.72
24 **Sheraton Fiji Resort** 75.36
25 **Stamford Plaza** Auckland 74.64

No. 18
HAYMAN, GREAT BARRIER
REEF, AUSTRALIA

The rooftop
terrace of
a beachfront
casita at
Mandarin Oriental
Riviera Maya.

HOTELS DIRECTORY

Kauai
Oahu
Lanai ——— Maui
Big Island

HAWAII

Whistler

VANCOUVER
ISLAND

Lake Louise
Banff

VANCOUVER AREA

Seattle

Portland

Darby

Jackson Hole

Park City

NAPA/SONOMA

San Francisco

Beaver Creek
Vail
Denver
Aspen

Pebble Beach

Carmel

Colorado Spring

Big Sur

Las Vegas

Santa Barbara

Sedona

LOS ANGELES AREA

Santa Fe

ORANGE COUNTY

PHOENIX/
SCOTTSDALE

SAN DIEGO AREA

Globe

Tucson

UNITED STATES +
CANADA

Quebec City ●

● Dixville Notch

ADIRONDACKS

● Boston
●── CAPE COD
● Nantucket
●── Montauk
●── New York City

Niagara-on-the-Lake ●

Kohler ●

Chicago ●

● Farmington

Philadelphia ●

Washington, D.C.
McLean ● ──
● ── Washington

White Sulphur Springs ●

Nashville ●   Walland ●
● Asheville

Greensboro ●

●── Charleston
● Kiawah Island

Dallas

● Sea Island

Austin

● Ponte Vedra Beach

Santa Rosa Beach

●── Orlando

New Orleans

● Palm Beach

Naples ●   ●── MIAMI AREA

FLORIDA KEYS

ARIZONA

GLOBE

Noftsger Hill Inn Bed & Breakfast Converted 1907 schoolhouse in a historic mining town. 877/780-2479 or 928/425-2260; noftsgerhillinn.com; doubles from $

PHOENIX/SCOTTSDALE

Hyatt Regency Resort & Spa at Gainey Ranch A top-notch spa, 3 golf courses, and mountain views on a 560-acre spread. Scottsdale; 800/233-1234 or 480/444-1234; hyatt.com; doubles from $

The Phoenician Opulent 250-acre resort (9 pools, 12 tennis courts, 27 holes of golf) on the south side of Camelback Mountain. Scottsdale; 800/325-3589 or 480/941-8200; the phoenician.com; doubles from $$$$

Royal Palms Resort & Spa 1929 Spanish colonial-style mansion with gardens and antiques-filled rooms. Phoenix; 800/672-6011 or 602/840-3610; royalpalmshotel.com; doubles from $$

Sanctuary on Camelback Mountain Resort & Spa Whitewashed adobe casitas with contemporary interiors. Paradise Valley; 800/245-2051 or 480/948-2100; sanctuaryaz.com; doubles from $$

SEDONA

Enchantment Resort Southwestern-style property inside a stunning red-rock canyon; the spa, Mii Amo, is one of the country's best. 800/826-4180 or 928/282-2900; enchantmentresort.com; doubles from $$

TUCSON

Arizona Inn 1930's adobe-style casitas with extensive manicured grounds. 2200 E. Elm St.; 800/933-1093 or 520/325-1541; arizonainn.com; doubles from $$

CALIFORNIA

BIG SUR

Post Ranch Inn Glass-walled suites and stone- and redwood cottages with cliffside views of the Pacific. 800/527-2200 or 831/667-2200; postranch inn.com; doubles from $$$, including breakfast

Ventana Inn & Spa A clutch of cedar lodges on 243 wooded acres, plus one of the area's top spas. 800/628-6500 or 831/667-2331; ventanainn. com; doubles from $$$, including breakfast

CARMEL

Bernardus Lodge Romantic Mediterranean-style resort (featherbeds, in-room fireplaces), surrounded by vineyards. 888/648-9463 or 831/658-3400; bernardus.com; doubles from $$$

LOS ANGELES AREA

Beverly Hills Hotel & Bungalows Mission-style "Pink Palace" with an Old Hollywood vibe. 9641 Sunset Blvd., Beverly Hills; 800/283-8885 or 310/276-2251; beverly hillshotel.com; doubles from $$$

Beverly Wilshire, A Four Seasons Hotel Legendary 1928 hotel with a prime location: the intersection of Rodeo Drive and Wilshire Boulevard. 9500 Wilshire Blvd., Beverly Hills; 800/332-3442 or 310/275-5200; fourseasons.com; doubles from $$$

Hotel Bel-Air Idyllic 12-acre hideaway in a residential neighborhood. 701 Stone Canyon Rd., Los Angeles; 800/648-4097 or 310/472-1211; hotelbelair.com; doubles from $$

Langham, Huntington Hotel & Spa 1907 landmark (formerly the Ritz-Carlton) at the base of the San Gabriel Mountains. 1401 S. Oak Knoll Ave., Pasadena; 800/588-9141 or 626/568-3900; langhamhotels.com; doubles from $$

Peninsula Beverly Hills Swank urban resort with an outdoor pool overlooking the L.A. skyline. 9882 S. Santa Monica Blvd., Beverly Hills; 800/462-7899 or 310/551-2888; peninsula.com; doubles from $$$

Shutters on the Beach Nantucket-style property, centrally located along Santa Monica Beach. 1 Pico Blvd., Santa Monica; 800/334-9000 or 310/458-0030; shutterson thebeach.com; doubles from $$$

Thompson Beverly Hills Popular new outpost with a buzzy late-night scene; interiors have a 70's-era flair. 9360 Wilshire Blvd., Beverly Hills; 800/441-5050 or 310/273-1400; thompsonhotels.com; doubles from $$

Viceroy Santa Monica Oceanside hotel near the Santa Monica Pier, with Hollywood Regency-inspired interiors. 1819 Ocean Ave., Santa Monica; 866/891-0947 or 310/260-7500; viceroysantamonica. com; doubles from $$

The pool at Calistoga Ranch's spa, in California's Napa Valley.

The iconic turret of San Diego's Hotel del Coronado.

NAPA/SONOMA

Auberge du Soleil Provençal-inspired inn on 33 olive grove- and vineyard-filled acres. Rutherford; 800/348-5406 or 707/963-1211; aubergedusoleil.com; doubles from $$$

Calistoga Ranch Sleek cottages in a secluded canyon overlooking the Mayacamas Mountains. Calistoga; 800/942-4220 or 707/254-2800; calistogaranch.com; doubles from $$$$

Hotel Healdsburg Urbane country inn co-owned by chef Charlie Palmer. Healdsburg; 800/889-7188 or 707/431-2800; hotelhealdsburg.com; doubles from $$

ORANGE COUNTY

Montage Laguna Beach Arts & Crafts-style decor in a dramatic bluff-top location. Laguna Beach; 888/715-6700 or 949/715-6000; montagelagunabeach.com; doubles from $$$

Ritz-Carlton, Laguna Niguel Pacific-front property with classic Ritz polish. Dana Point; 800/241-3333 or 949/240-2000; ritzcarlton.com; doubles from $$

St. Regis Monarch Beach Tuscan-inspired resort with Dale Chihuly sculptures. Dana Point; 877/787-3447 or 949/234-3200; stregis.com; doubles from $$$

PEBBLE BEACH

Inn at Spanish Bay Hacienda-like oasis on the Monterey Peninsula; guests have full golf privileges at the Pebble Beach courses. 800/654-9300 or 831/647-7500; pebblebeach.com; doubles from $$$

Lodge at Pebble Beach Traditional 1919 resort with a prime location on the Pebble Beach Golf Links. 800/654-9300 or 831/624-3811; pebblebeach.com; doubles from $$$

SAN DIEGO AREA

Cal-a-Vie Terra-cotta-roofed cottages and a wellness center in 200 forested acres. Vista; 866/772-4283 or 760/945-2055; cal-a-vie.com; doubles from $$$$$, all-inclusive

Chopra Center for Wellbeing at La Costa Resort & Spa Deepak Chopra-led spa that combines Western and Eastern philosophies, on a 400-acre resort. Carlsbad; 888/424-6772 or 760/494-1639; chopra.com; doubles from $

Four Seasons Resort Aviara Spanish colonial-style property with the area's only Arnold Palmer-designed golf course and easy access to the beach. Carlsbad; 800/332-3442 or 760/603-6800; fourseasons.com; doubles from $$

Golden Door Legendary SoCal spa with a full roster of beauty and health programs. Escondido; 800/424-0777 or 760/744-5777; goldendoor.com; $$$$$, all-inclusive, one-week minimum

Hotel del Coronado Storied 1888 Victorian resort on 28 oceanfront acres. Coronado; 866/468-3533 or 619/435-6611; hoteldel.com; doubles from $$

Lodge at Torrey Pines Craftsman-inspired resort on the Torrey Pines Golf Course; interiors feature William Morris wallpaper and Stickley furniture. La Jolla; 800/656-0087 or 858/453-4420; lodgetorreypines.com; doubles from $$

SAN FRANCISCO
Four Seasons Hotel Glass high-rise in the Yerba Buena district. 757 Market St.; 800/332-3442 or 415/633-3000; fourseasons.com; doubles from $$

Mandarin Oriental On the top 11 floors of a Financial District tower, with sweeping city views. 222 Sansome St.; 800/526-6566 or 415/276-9888; mandarinoriental.com; doubles from $$$

Ritz-Carlton 100-year-old Neoclassical hotel in Nob Hill. 600 Stockton St.; 800/241-3333 or 415/296-7465; ritzcarlton.com; doubles from $$

SANTA BARBARA
Canary Hotel Moorish-influenced details at a just-opened downtown hotel. 877/468-3515 or 805/884-0300; canarysantabarbara.com; doubles from $$

Four Seasons Resort, The Biltmore 1927 grande dame with a private beach club. Montecito; 800/332-3442 or 805/969-2261; fourseasons.com; doubles from $$$

COLORADO
ASPEN
Little Nell Ski-in, ski-out resort, with David Easton-designed interiors and *the* après-ski scene. 888/843-6355 or 970/920-4600; thelittlenell.com; doubles from $$$

BEAVER CREEK
Park Hyatt Resort & Spa Contemporary lodge in the heart of Beaver Creek Village. 800/233-1234 or 970/949-1234; park.hyatt.com; doubles from $$$

Ritz-Carlton, Bachelor Gulch Western-style timbered lodge with a

21,000-square-foot spa; a chairlift is right out the door. 800/241-3333 or 970/748-6200; ritzcarlton.com; doubles from $$$

COLORADO SPRINGS
The Broadmoor Italianate lakeside resort with loads of outdoor activities. 866/837-9520 or 719/634-7711; broadmoor.com; doubles from $$

DENVER
Hotel Teatro Renaissance Revival property across from the Denver Center for the Performing Arts. 1100 14th St.; 888/727-1200 or 303/228-1100; hotelteatro.com; doubles from $$

VAIL
Tivoli Lodge Alps-inspired lodge that's just undergone a $30 million renovation. 800/451-4756 or 970/476-5615; tivolilodge.com; doubles from $$

CONNECTICUT
WASHINGTON
Mayflower Inn & Spa Country estate with a 20,000-square-foot spa. 860/868-9466; mayflowerinn.com; doubles from $$$$$, all-inclusive

DISTRICT OF COLUMBIA
WASHINGTON, D.C.
Donovan House Design-

forward hotel with a hot-spot rooftop pool. 1155 14th St. NW; 800/383-6900 or 202/737-1200; thompsonhotels.com; doubles from $$

The Hay-Adams 1928 landmark with Thomas Pheasant-designed interiors, across from the White House. 1 Lafayette Square; 800/853-6807 or 202/638-6600; hayadams.com; doubles from $$

Ritz-Carlton, Georgetown Cosmopolitan property overlooking the Potomac River. 3100 South St. NW; 800/241-3333 or 202/912-4100; ritzcarlton.com; doubles from $$$$

Sofitel Lafayette Square Art-filled 1886 limestone building with bold Pierre-Yves Rochon-designed interiors. 806 15th St. NW; 800/763-4835 or202/730-8800; sofitel.com; doubles from $$

FLORIDA
FLORIDA KEYS
Azul del Mar Six-room villa on a secluded beach. Key Largo; 888/253-2985 or 305/451-0337; azulhotels.us; doubles from $

Little Palm Island Resort & Spa South Seas–style retreat on a private 6-acre island. Little Torch Key;

800/343-8567 or 305/872-2524; littlepalmisland.com; doubles from $$$$

MIAMI

Four Seasons Hotel Twelve floors of a glass-and-granite high-rise in the heart of the business district. 1435 Brickell Ave.; 800/332-3442 or 305/358-3535; fourseasons.com; doubles from $$$

Gansevoort South Beautifully restored Art Deco hotel; the sprawling rooftop is one of South Beach's most popular clubs. 2377 Collins Ave.; 305/604-1000; gansevoortsouth.com; doubles from $$$

Tides South Beach Kelly Wearstler-designed hotel with a Palm Beach-revisited vibe. 1220 Ocean Dr.; 800/439-4095 or 305/604-5070; tidessouthbeach.com; doubles from $$$

NAPLES

Ritz-Carlton Beachfront Mediterranean-style property (the flagship Ritz-Carlton resort) that's both sophisticated and family-friendly; guests have access to some of the state's best golf (at its sister property, below). 800/241-3333 or 239/598-3300; ritzcarlton.com; doubles from $$$

Ritz-Carlton Golf Resort Inland resort with 2 Greg Norman–designed courses; it's sportier and more informal than the beachfront Ritz (see above). 800/241-3333 or 239/593-2000; ritzcarlton.com; doubles from $$

ORLANDO

Ritz-Carlton, Grande Lakes Orlando's most luxurious property: an opulent 14-story tower, with a Greg Norman–designed golf course and a 40,000-square-foot spa. 800/241-3333 or 407/206-2400; ritzcarlton.com; doubles from $$

PALM BEACH

The Breakers Oceanfront grande dame modeled on Rome's Villa Medici. 888/273-2537 or 561/655-6611; thebreakers.com; doubles from $$$

Four Seasons Resort Glass-and-stucco low-rise on the ocean with a new 11,000-square-foot spa. 800/332-3442 or 561/582-2800; fourseasons.com; doubles from $$$

PONTE VEDRA

Lodge & Club at Ponte Vedra Mediterranean-style compound on 10 acres, plus access to the facilities at its sister property (see below).

800/243-4304 or 904/273-9500; pvresorts.com; doubles from $$

Ponte Vedra Inn & Club 80-year-old golf and tennis resort on 300 oceanfront acres with a recently completed 30,000-square-foot spa. 800/234-7842 or 904/285-1111; pvresorts.com; doubles from $$

SANTA ROSA BEACH

WaterColor Inn & Resort David Rockwell–designed beachfront hotel in a Panhandle development. 866/426-2656 or 850/534-5000; watercolorresort.com; doubles from $$

GEORGIA

GREENSBORO

Ritz-Carlton Lodge, Reynolds Plantation Cedar-shingled lakeside lodge and cottages, 75 miles east of Atlanta. 800/241-3333 or 706/467-0600; ritzcarlton.com; doubles from $$

SEA ISLAND

The Cloister Addison Mizner–inspired spread with 149 rooms on a private barrier island; facilities include 3 golf courses and an equestrian center. 888/732-4752 or 912/638-3611; seaisland.com; doubles from $$$$

HAWAII

BIG ISLAND

Fairmont Orchid Pair of oceanfront towers on a sheltered Kohala Coast bay. 800/441-1414 or 808/885-2000; fairmont.com; doubles from $$

Four Seasons Resort Hualalai Bungalow-style, family-friendly resort on the rocky north Kona Coast. 800/332-3442 or 808/325-8000; fourseasons.com; doubles from $$$$

Mauna Kea Beach Hotel Open-air retreat on a dazzling Kaunaoa Bay beach; home to a famed Robert Trent Jones Sr.-designed golf course. 866/774-6236 or 808/882-7222; princeresortshawaii.com; doubles from $$

Mauna Lani Bay Hotel & Bungalows Low-rise hotel on secluded Kohala Coast shoreline with a 40,000-square-foot spa. 800/367-2323 or 808/885-6622; maunalani.com; doubles from $$

Waikoloa Beach Marriott Resort & Spa Oceanfront Kohala Coast property that recently completed a $54 million renovation. 800/228-9290 or 808/886-6789; marriott.com; doubles from $$

KAUAI

Grand Hyatt Resort & Spa
Sprawling, plantation-style resort on the south shore's Shipwreck Beach. 800/233-1234 or 808/742-1234; grandhyatt.com; doubles from $$

Kauai Marriott Resort & Beach Club Expansive, convention-friendly hotel on 800 acres, located between the north and south shores. 800/228-9290 or 808/245-5050; marriott.com; doubles from $$

The Orchids restaurant at Halekulani, in Honolulu.

Princeville Resort Three terraced buildings overlooking Hanalei Bay; closed until April; recently converted to a St. Regis property. 800/325-3589 or 808/826-9644; princeville.com

LANAI

Four Seasons Resort Lanai at Manele Bay
Asian-inspired cliffside resort on Hulopoe Bay, a protected marine reserve. 800/332-3442 or 808/565-2000; fourseasons.com; doubles from $$

Four Seasons Resort Lanai, The Lodge at Koele Elegant country house offering a unique highlands experience, with hunting, horseback riding, and a Greg Norman–designed course. 800/332-3442 or 808/565-4000; fourseasons.com; doubles from $$

MAUI

Fairmont Kea Lani
Moorish-style property on 22 oceanfront acres adjacent to Polo Beach. 800/441-1414 or 808/875-4100; fairmont.com; doubles from $$$

Four Seasons Resort Maui at Wailea Garden paradise on one of Maui's best beaches, with a host of free activities (canoe excursions, snorkeling). 800/332-3443 or 808/874-8000; fourseasons.com; doubles from $$$

Grand Wailea Resort Hotel & Spa Posh family-friendly resort on 40 acres of Maui's southeastern coast. 800/888-6100 or 808/875-1234; grandwailea.com; doubles from $$$

Hotel Hana-Maui & Honua Spa Secluded cottages offering a total escape (no in-room TV's, radios, or alarm clocks).

800/321-4262 or 808/248-8211; hotelhanamaui.com; doubles from $$

Ritz-Carlton, Kapalua
Oceanfront resort fresh from a $180 million redo, flanked by two golf courses. 800/241-3333 or 808/669-6200; ritzcarlton.com; doubles from $$

Sheraton Maui Resort & Spa On Kaanapali's Black Rock, 508 rooms and a host of activities. 800/325-3535 or 808/661-0031; sheraton.com; doubles from $$$

Wailea Beach Marriott Resort & Spa Waterslides and a luau, a quick oceanside stroll from Mokapu Beach Park. 888/236-2477 or 808/879-1922; marriott.com; doubles from $$$

Westin Resort & Spa Kaanapali U-shaped complex with five pools and multiple activity options (scuba diving, hula classes). 866/716-8140 or 808/667-2525; westin.com; doubles from $$$

OAHU

Halekulani Five interconnected buildings surrounded by gardens; the views of Diamond Head and Waikiki Beach are spectacular. 800/367-2343 or

A guest-room
terrace at the
Peninsula
Chicago.

808/923-2311; halekulani.com; doubles from $$

Hyatt Regency Waikiki Beach Resort & Spa
Two 40-story towers in the heart of Waikiki, steps from more than 60 boutiques. 800/233-1234 or 808/923-1234; hyatt.com; doubles from $$

JW Marriott Ihilani Resort & Spa Terraced 17-story hotel at the edge of a lagoon in Ko Olina Resort & Marina. 800/228-9290 or 808/679-0079; ihilani.com; doubles from $$

Kahala Hotel & Resort Plantation-style resort fresh from a $50 million renovation. 800/367-2525 or 808/739-8888; kahala resort.com; doubles from $$

Moana Surfrider, A Westin Resort & Spa Meticulously restored 1901 Beaux-Arts property with an Old Hawaii vibe and an oceanfront spa. 800/228-3000 or 808/922-3111; moana-surfrider.com; doubles from $$

Royal Hawaiian Pink palazzo-style Waikiki Beach icon; the pool is brand-new. 800/325-3589 or 808/923-7311; royal-hawaiian.com; doubles from $$$

Turtle Bay Resort The North Shore's only luxury resort; a surfing school, horse stables, and a 36-hole golf course. 800/203-3650 or 808/293-6000; turtlebayresort.com; doubles from $$

ILLINOIS
CHICAGO
Four Seasons Floors 30–46 of a Michigan Avenue sky-scraper with dramatic city views from every room. 120 E. Delaware Place; 800/332-3442 or 312/280-8800; fourseasons.com; doubles from $$

The James Loft-style hotel one block west of Michigan Avenue. 55 E. Ontario St.; 877/526-3755 or 312/337-1000; jameshotels.com; doubles from $$

Peninsula Chicago 20-story tower with two excellent restaurants: Avenues and Shanghai Terrace. 108 E. Superior St.; 866/382-8388 or 312/337-2888; peninsula.com; doubles from $$$

Ritz-Carlton, A Four Seasons Hotel Sumptuous hotel occupying 21 floors of a high-rise. 160 E. Pearson St.; 800/332-3442 or 312/266-1000; fourseasons.com; doubles from $$

LOUISIANA
NEW ORLEANS
Windsor Court Hotel Refined 23-story hotel in the business district. 300 Gravier St.; 800/237-1238 or 504/523-6000; windsor courthotel.com; doubles from $$

MASSACHUSETTS
BOSTON
Eliot Hotel 1925 property that has two top-notch res-taurants and a convenient Back Bay location. 370 Commonwealth Ave.; 800/443-5468 or 617/267-1607; eliothotel.com; doubles from $$

XV Beacon Handsome contemporary Beacon Hill hotel in a 1903 Beaux-Arts building. 15 Beacon St.; 877/982-3226 or 617/670-1500; xvbeacon.com; doubles from $$

Four Seasons Hotel Dignified red-brick hotel facing the Boston Common and Public Gardens. 200 Boylston St.; 800/332-3442 or 617/338-4400; fourseasons.com; doubles from $$

Jurys Boston Italian Renaissance Revival building transformed into a chic urban retreat in the heart of the Back Bay. 350 Stuart St.; 617/532-3800;

jurysdoyle.com; doubles from $$

Liberty Hotel Downtown property in a converted jail, with Alexandra Champalimaud–designed interiors and a restaurant from Lydia Shire. 215 Charles St.; 866/507-5245 or 617/224-4000; libertyhotel.com; doubles from $$$

CAPE COD
Chatham Bars Inn 1914 grande-dame resort that's the quintessential New England seaside retreat. 800/223-6800 or 508/945-0096; chatham barsinn.com; doubles from $$

NANTUCKET
The Wauwinet Posh and classic shingled inn set between Nantucket Harbor and the Atlantic Ocean. 800/426-8718 or 508/228-0145; wauwinet.com; doubles from $$$

MONTANA
DARBY
Triple Creek Ranch Luxe log cabins with excellent service and food and a comprehensive range of activities (cattle drives, fly-fishing). 800/654-2943 or 406/821-4600; triplecreekranch.com; doubles from $$$, all-inclusive

NEVADA
LAS VEGAS

The Bellagio Italianate extravaganza in the middle of the Strip with first-rate dining. 3600 Las Vegas Blvd. S.; 888/987-6667 or 702/693-7111; bellagio.com; doubles from $

Flamingo Las Vegas Fabled Vegas mainstay with 1,032 just-refreshed retro-chic rooms. 3555 Las Vegas Blvd. S.; 800/732-2111 or 702/733-3111; flamingovegas.com; doubles from $

Four Seasons Hotel Floors 35-39 of the Mandalay Bay tower, on the Strip's south end; the city's most understated hotel. 3960 Las Vegas Blvd. S.; 800/332-3442 or 702/632-5000; fourseasons.com; doubles from $$

Wynn Las Vegas Sophisticated Strip hotel with a golf course and a casino flooded with natural light. 3131 Las Vegas Blvd. S.; 877/321-9966 or 702/770-7000; wynnlasvegas. com; doubles from $$

NEW HAMPSHIRE
DIXVILLE NOTCH

Balsams Grand Resort Hotel White Mountains retreat with lovely Victorian buildings and loads of activities (kayaking, mountain biking). 800/255-0600 or 603/255-3400; thebalsams.com; doubles from $$

NEW MEXICO
SANTA FE

Inn of the Anasazi, A Rosewood Hotel Authentic, Southwestern-style hotel steps from the historic plaza. 888/767-3966 or 505/988-3030; innof theanasazi.com; doubles from $$

NEW YORK
LAKE PLACID

Lake Placid Lodge Recently restored 1882 lakeside resort with featherbeds and handcrafted "twig" furniture. 877/523-2700 or 518/523-2700; lakeplacidlodge. com; doubles from $$$$, including breakfast and afternoon tea

Mirror Lake Inn Resort & Spa Family-friendly lodge with a cozy vibe, only one block from downtown. 518/523-2544; mirrorlakeinn. com; doubles from $$

MONTAUK

Surf Lodge Laid-back beach retreat that has a happening bar scene and restaurant. 631/668-2632; thesurflodge. com; doubles from $$, two-night minimum

Four Seasons Hotel I. M. Pei-designed midtown tower with one of Joël Robuchon's L'Atelier restaurants. 57 E. 57th St.; 800/332-3442 or 212/758-5700; fourseasons.com; doubles from $$$$

Greenwich Hotel Robert De Niro's latest venture, in fashionable TriBeCa. 377 Greenwich St.; 212-941-8900; thegreenwichhotel. com; doubles from $$

Mandarin Oriental Floors 35-54 of the Time Warner Center, steps from Central Park. 80 Columbus Circle; 866/801-8880 or 212/805-8800; mandarin oriental.com; doubles from $$$$

Ritz-Carlton Central Park Limestone building with a gracious townhouse feel, right across from Central Park. 50 Central Park S.; 800/241-3333 or 212/308-9100; ritzcarlton.com; doubles from $$$$

The Royalton Iconic 1988 property with thoroughly transformed public spaces, thanks to New York City-based Roman & Williams. 44 W. 44th St.; 800/635-9013 or 212/869-4400; royaltonhotel.com; doubles from $$$

St. Regis 1904 Beaux-Arts landmark; opulent details include Waterford crystal chandeliers and Alain Ducasse's Adour restaurant. 2 E. 55th St.; 877/787-3447 or 212/753-4500; stregis.com; doubles from $$$$

NORTH CAROLINA
ASHEVILLE

Inn on Biltmore Estate Manor house adjacent to the Biltmore House, George Vanderbilt's 19th-century château. 800/411-3812 or 828/225-1600; biltmore. com; doubles from $$

OREGON
PORTLAND

Ace Hotel Vintage touches and a rock'n'roll vibe that caters to the creative class. 1022 SW Stark St.; 503/228-2277; acehotel.com; doubles from $

Hotel Vintage Plaza Historic red-brick 1894 hotel in the heart of downtown. 422 SW Broadway; 800/263-2305 or 503/228-1212; vintageplaza.com; doubles from $

PENNSYLVANIA
FARMINGTON

Nemacolin Woodlands Resort Compound on 3,000 acres with activities from bowling to skeet shooting. 800/422-2736 or

724/329-8555; nemacolin.
com; doubles from $

Four Seasons Hotel Eight-
story granite property
located in the city's cultural
center. 1 Logan Square;
800/332-3442 or 215/963-
1500; fourseasons.com;
doubles from $$

Rittenhouse Hotel
Distinguished hotel in a
lively downtown neighbor-
hood. 210 W. Rittenhouse
Sq.; 800/635-1042 or 215/
546-9000; rittenhouse
hotel.com; doubles from $$

SOUTH CAROLINA
CHARLESTON
Charleston Place Georgian-
style property in the historic
district. 205 Meeting St.;
800/611-5545 or 843/722-
4900; charlestonplace.com;
doubles from $$

Planters Inn Gracious
retreat on the edge of the
City Market. 112 N. Market
St.; 800/845-7082 or
843/722-2345; planters
inn.com; doubles from $$

KIAWAH ISLAND
**Sanctuary at Kiawah
Island Golf Resort**
Oceanside estate with
world-class golf and tennis
facilities on a barrier
island 30 minutes south
of Charleston. 877/683-1234

or 843/768-6000; kiawah
resort.com; doubles from $$

TENNESSEE
NASHVILLE
Hermitage Hotel
Beaux-Arts property that's
the hotel of choice for
country music stars. 231
6th Ave. N.; 888/ 888-
9414 or 615/244-3121;
thehermitagehotel.com;
doubles from $

WALLAND
Blackberry Farm Pastoral
estate in the Great Smoky
Mountain foothills. 800/
273-6004 or 865/984-
8166; blackberryfarm.com;
doubles from $$$,
all-inclusive

TEXAS
AUSTIN
Hotel San José Spanish
colonial-style former motel

in the trendy South
Congress district. 1316 S.
Congress Ave.; 800/574-
8897 or 512/444-7322;
sanjosehotel.com; doubles
from $

DALLAS
**Four Seasons Resort &
Club Dallas at Las Colinas**
Sprawling development
with 2 golf courses, 4 pools,
and a 6,000-square-foot

The Greenwich
Hotel's lobby, in
New York City.

The courtyard pool at Austin's Hotel San José.

fitness center. 4150 N. MacArthur Blvd.; 800/332-3442 or 972/717-0700; fourseasons.com; doubles from $$

UTAH
PARK CITY
Stein Eriksen Lodge Scandinavian-inspired chalet with cathedral ceilings and whirlpool tubs in every room. 800/453-1302 or 435/649-3700; steinlodge.com; doubles from $$$$

VIRGINIA
MCLEAN
Ritz-Carlton, Tysons Corner Steps from great shopping, across the Potomac from D.C. 800/241-3333 or 703/506-4300; ritzcarlton.com; doubles from $$

WASHINGTON
Inn at Little Washington Romantic country retreat; owner Patrick O'Connell's restaurant is a destination in itself. 800/735-2478 or 540/675-3800; theinn atlittlewashington.com; doubles from $$$

WASHINGTON
SEATTLE
Inn at the Market Handsome brick building with an ivy-draped court-yard; the only hotel in Pike Place Market.

KEY TO THE PRICE ICONS $ UNDER $250 $$ $250-$499 $$$ $500-$749 $$$$ $750-$999 $$$$$ $1,000 AND UP

86 Pine St.; 800/446-4484 or 206/443-3600; innatthemarket.com; doubles from $

WEST VIRGINIA
WHITE SULPHUR SPRINGS
The Greenbrier Formal, historic resort in the Allegheny Mountains, renowned for its Dorothy Draper interiors. 800/453-4858 or 304/536-1110; greenbrier.com; doubles from $$

WISCONSIN
KOHLER
American Club at Destination Kohler Tudor-style 1918 building on the Sheboygan River; it has the area's best spa. 800/344-2838 or 920/457-8000; destination kohler.com; doubles from $$

WYOMING
JACKSON HOLE
Four Seasons Resort Alpine retreat with ski-in, ski-out access. 800/332-3442 or 307/732-5000; fourseasons. com; doubles from $$$

Hotel Terra Upscale, eco-conscious ski lodge. 800/631-6281 or 307/739-4000; hotelterrajacksonhole.com; doubles from $

Rusty Parrot Lodge & Spa Gabled lodgepole-pine inn on Miller Park. 888/739-1749 or 307/733-2000; rustyparrot.com; doubles from $$

ALBERTA
BANFF
Rimrock Resort Hotel Ten-story mountaintop lodge, a short drive from the Banff Gondola. 888/746-7625 or 403/762-3356; rimrockresort.com; doubles from $$

LAKE LOUISE
Fairmont Château Lake Louise European-style resort dating from 1892 with views of Victoria Glacier. 800/441-1414 or 403/522-3511; fairmont. com; doubles from $$

Post Hotel & Spa Tranquil 1942 lodge along the Pipestone River; family-owned and -operated. 800/661-1586 or 403/522-3989; posthotel.com; doubles from $$

BRITISH COLUMBIA
VANCOUVER AREA
Fairmont Vancouver Airport Modern 392-room annex at Vancouver International Airport, 30 minutes from the city. 800/441-1414 or 604/207-5200; fairmont. com; doubles from $$

Four Seasons Hotel The city's largest luxury rooms, in a 28-story downtown high-rise. 791 W. Georgia St.; 800/332-3442 or 604/689-9333; fourseasons. com; doubles from $$

Metropolitan Hotel Financial District tower with a three-hole putting green. 645 Howe St.; 800/667-2300 or 604/687-1122; metropolitan. com; doubles from $$

Wedgewood Hotel & Spa Cultivated downtown property filled with art from the owners' private collection. 845 Hornby St.; 800/663-0666 or 604/689-7777; wedgewoodhotel.com; doubles from $$

VANCOUVER ISLAND
Clayoquot Wilderness Resort 20 antiques-filled tents on a bay accessible only by boat or floatplane. 888/333-5405 or 250/726-8235; wildretreat. com; doubles from $$$$, three-night minimum, all-inclusive

Wickaninnish Inn Cedar lodge with handmade driftwood furniture and an excellent spa, on a pine forest-ringed promontory. Tofino; 800/333-4604 or 250/725-3100; wickinn. com; doubles from $$

WHISTLER
Fairmont Château Whistler Ski-in, ski-out resort fresh from a $13 million upgrade. 800/441-1414 or 604/938-8000; fairmont.com; doubles from $$

Four Seasons Resort Rustic-chic lodge that's a five-minute walk from Blackcomb Mountain. 800/332-3442 or 604/935-3400; fourseasons. com; doubles from $$

ONTARIO
NIAGARA-ON-THE-LAKE
Prince of Wales 1864 Victorian mansion in the town's historic center. 888/669-5566 or 905/468-3246; vintage-hotels.com; doubles from $$

QUEBEC
QUEBEC CITY
Auberge Saint-Antoine Collection of classic and contemporary buildings, adjacent to the Musée de la Civilisation. 8 Rue St.-Antoine; 888/692-2211 or 418/692-2211; saint-antoine. com; doubles from $$

Fairmont Le Château Frontenac 1893 landmark above the St. Lawrence River, within the walls of Old Quebec. 1 Rue des Carrières; 800/441-1414 or 418/692-3861; fairmont. com; doubles from $$

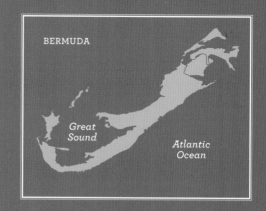

THE BAHAMAS

Atlantic Ocean

TURKS AND CAICOS

DOMINICAN REPUBLIC

ST. THOMAS

CAYMAN ISLANDS

PUERTO RICO

ST. JOHN
PETER ISLAND

JAMAICA

ANGUILLA
VIRGIN
GORDA
ST. MARTIN
SABA

ST. CROIX
NEVIS
ANTIGUA

Caribbean Sea

ST. LUCIA

ARUBA

CARIBBEAN +
THE BAHAMAS +
BERMUDA

ANGUILLA

Cap Juluca Moorish-style buildings along 179 acres of secluded Maundays Bay Beach, only 25 minutes by boat from busy St. Martin. 888/858-5822 or 264/497-6666; capjuluca.com; doubles from $$$$

CuisinArt Resort & Spa Mediterranean-inspired villas and a standout spa (16 treatment rooms, including dual hammams) on a bend of Rendezvous Bay. 800/943-3210 or 264/498-2000; cuisinartresort.com; doubles from $$$

ANTIGUA

Sandals Grande Resort & Spa Terra-cotta-roofed bungalows on the powdery beach at Dickenson Bay. 800/726-3257 or 268/462-0267; sandals.com; doubles from $$$$, all-inclusive

ARUBA

Hyatt Regency Resort & Casino Oceanfront compound with 360 rooms and a 5,000-square-foot freshwater lagoon. 800/233-1234 or 297/586-1234; hyatt.com; doubles from $$$

Radisson Resort, Casino & Spa Three-tower Dutch Colonial resort and casino with Aruba's most comprehensive spa. 800/333-3333 or 011-297/586-6555; radisson.com; doubles from $$

BAHAMAS

Four Seasons Resort Great Exuma at Emerald Bay Low-slung pastel buildings on a 470-acre oceanfront spread. Great Exuma; 800/332-3442 or 242/336-6800; fourseasons.com; doubles from $$$

The Landing Aristocratic 7-room inn with an excellent restaurant, near the ferry dock. Harbour Island; 242/333-2707; harbourislandlanding.com; doubles from $$

One & Only Ocean Club Lavish British colonial oceanfront plantation; the surrounding Versailles-like gardens were purchased from William Randolph Hearst. Paradise Island; 800/321-3000 or 242/363-2501; oneandonlyresorts.com; doubles from $$$

Pink Sands Storied retro-chic property recently refreshed by Barbara Hulanicki, overlooking a pink-sand beach. Harbour Island; 800/407-4776 or 242/333-2030; pinksandsresort.com; doubles from $$$$

Tiamo Eco-focused, laid-back resort; staff biologists lead snorkeling excursions. South Andros Island; 242/369-2330; tiamoresorts.com; doubles from $$$$, including meals

BERMUDA

Elbow Beach Historic 50-acre, garden-filled resort, recently purchased by Mandarin Oriental. 800/223-7434 or 441/236-3535; mandarinoriental.com; doubles from $$

Fairmont Southampton Coral-pink hotel with traditional interiors and spacious guest rooms. 800/441-1414 or 441/238-8000; fairmont.com; doubles from $$

The Reefs Salmon-limestone hotel on a South Shore cliff. 800/742-2008 or 441/238-0222; thereefs.com; doubles from $$$, including breakfast and dinner

CAYMAN ISLANDS

Ritz-Carlton, Grand Cayman Oceanside resort on 144 acres fronting Seven Mile Beach; amenities include a Jean-Michel Cousteau children's program and a La Prairie spa. 800/241-3333 or 345/943-9000; ritzcarlton.com; doubles from $$$

DOMINICAN REPUBLIC

Casa de Campo Vegas-style grandeur on the southeastern coast, with an equestrian center, yacht club, and expansive new spa. 800/877-3643 or 809/523-3333; casadecampo.com.do; doubles from $$

Puntacana Resort & Club Sprawling 15,000-acre complex that includes newly refurbished casitas and Tortuga Bay, a smaller property within the resort, designed by Oscar de la Renta. 888/442-2262 or 809/959-2262; puntacana.com; doubles at Puntacana from $; doubles at Tortuga Bay from $$$

JAMAICA

Couples Negril Enclave of 234 rooms with extensive activities that run the gamut from reggae-dancing lessons to croquet. 800/268-7537 or 876/957-5960; couples.com; doubles from $$$

Couples Swept Away Recently expanded, all-suite property on Seven Mile Beach; wellness facilities include an open-air gym, 82-foot lap pool, and new 4,500-square-foot spa. 800/268-7537 or 876/957-4061; couples.com; doubles from $$$

Goldeneye Exclusive lagoonside getaway made up of four villas and Ian

Fleming's onetime home. 800/688-7678 or 876/975-3354; goldeneyehotel.com; doubles from $$$$, all-inclusive

Grand Lido Negril Resort & Spa Ocean-facing suites and a full roster of activities (volleyball, waterskiing, diving). 800/467-8737 or 876/957-5010; superclubs.com; doubles from $$$

Half Moon Legendary estate on 400 acres, with polished service and a new 68,000-square-foot spa. 800/626-0592 or 876/953-2211; halfmoon.com; doubles from $$

Sandals Whitehouse European Village & Spa 50-acre complex on a secluded two-mile beach; interiors (dark-wood furniture, tapestries) are inspired by the Old World. 800/726-3257 or 876/640-3000; sandals.com; doubles from $$$$, all-inclusive

NEVIS
Four Seasons Resort Gingerbread-trimmed buildings next to Pinney's Beach. 800/332-3442 or 869/469-1111; fourseasons.com; doubles from $$$

Montpelier Plantation Inn Restored former sugar estate with 17 rooms. 869/469-3462; montpeliernevis.com; doubles from $$$

PETER ISLAND
Peter Island Resort Two-story bungalows on a 1,800-acre private island with beaches, hiking and biking trails, and prime diving sites. 800/346-4451 or 284/495-2000; peterisland.com; doubles from $$$$, including meals

PUERTO RICO
Hacienda Gripiñas 1858 plantation house converted to a comfortable inn. 787/828-1717; haciendagripinas.com; doubles from $

Horned Dorset Primavera Whitewashed stucco buildings fronting the beach, with 39 spacious suites. 800/633-1857 or 787/823-4030; horneddorset.com; doubles from $$$

Hotel El Convento Meticulously restored 1651 convent with beamed ceilings and tiled floors. 800/468-2779 or 787/723-9020; elconvento.com; doubles from $$

Ritz-Carlton Hotel, Spa & Casino Beachfront resort with Neoclassical interiors and some of San Juan's best restaurants (BLT Steak, Il Mulino). 800/

241-3333 or 787/253-1700; ritzcarlton.com; doubles from $$$

SABA
Queen's Gardens Resort Twelve-suite outpost at the base of lush Mount Scenery. 599/416-3494; queenssaba.com; doubles from $$

ST. CROIX
The Buccaneer 17th-century great house plus bungalows on a 340-acre estate. 800/255-3881 or 340/712-2100; thebuccaneer.com; doubles from $$, including breakfast and scuba classes

ST. JOHN
Caneel Bay, A Rosewood Resort Waterfront cottages on 7 separate beaches on a former sugar plantation. 888/767-3966 or 340/776-6111; caneelbay.com; doubles from $$$

ST. LUCIA
Sandals Grande St. Lucian Spa & Beach Resort British colonial–inspired enclave fronting the beach (guests can book swim-up rooms). 800/726-3257 or 758/455-2000; sandals.com; doubles from $$$$, all-inclusive

ST. MARTIN
Sol é Luna Inn Six uniquely decorated rooms adjoining a long-beloved restaurant in a residential neighborhood.

590-590/290-856; soleluna restaurant.com; doubles from $

ST. THOMAS
Ritz-Carlton Recently renovated complex on 33 oceanside acres; a great diving center. 800/241-3333 or 340/775-3333; ritzcarlton.com; doubles from $$$

TURKS AND CAICOS
Parrot Cay Trendsetting private-island resort with an Asian aesthetic on a 3-mile beach. 877/754-0726 or 649/946-7788; parrot cay.como.bz; doubles from $$$$, including transfers

VIRGIN GORDA
Biras Creek Collection of suites on a 140-acre peninsula framed by a white-sand beach and Berchers Bay. 877/883-0756 or 284/494-3555; biras.com; doubles from $$$$$, including meals

Bitter End Yacht Club Watersports-focused resort; beach villas have just been redone by Barbara Hulanicki. 800/872-2392; beyc.com; doubles from $$$$, all-inclusive

Rosewood Little Dix Bay Quiet, family-friendly resort on 500 oceanfront acres. 888/767-3966 or 284/495-5555; littledixbay.com; doubles from $$$$

KEY TO THE PRICE ICONS $ UNDER $250 $$ $250-$499 $$$ $500-$749 $$$$ $750-$999 $$$$$ $1,000 AND UP

A guest room at Montpelier Plantation Inn, on Nevis.

Los Cabos •

Mazatlán •

Punta Mita •
Mexico City •
Zihuatanejo •
Acapulco •
Oaxaca •

Holbox Island •
Cancún •
RIVIERA MAYA

Tikal •

Cartagena •

San Juan del Sur •
GUANACASTE

Bajos del Toro •

Panama City •

Lima •

Cuzco • • Machu Picchu

San Pedro de Atacama •

Rio de Janeiro •

Easter Island •

Santiago • Mendoza •

Buenos Aires •

San Carlos de Bariloche •

MEXICO + CENTRAL
+ SOUTH AMERICA

ARGENTINA
BUENOS AIRES
Alvear Palace 1932 grande dame in the heart of Recoleta, with an old-world feel and up-to-the-minute extras, such as La Prairie spa treatments. 1891 Avda. Alvear; 800/223-6800 or 54-11/4808-2100; alvearpalace.com; doubles from $$

The Cocker Quirky and welcoming 4-room hotel in the San Telmo district. 458 Juan de Garay; 54-11/4362-8451; thecocker.com; doubles from $, including breakfast

Four Seasons Hotel Belle Époque mansion and contemporary tower in Recoleta, featuring the excellent restaurant Le Mistral. 1086 Posadas; 800/332-3442 or 54-11/4321-1200; fourseasons.com; doubles from $$

MENDOZA
Park Hyatt 7-floor hotel with a restored Spanish-colonial façade and polished service, on downtown's Plaza Independencia. 800/233-1234 or 54-261/441-1234; park.hyatt.com; doubles from $$

SAN CARLOS DE BARILOCHE
Correntoso Lake & River Hotel Former fishing camp turned upscale lodge on the shores of Lake Nahuel Huapi. 54-11/4803-0030; correntoso.com; doubles from $$, including breakfast

Llao Llao Hotel & Resort Golf Spa Historic cypress-and-stone lodge in Nahuel Huapi National Park. 54-29/4444-8530; llaollao.com; doubles from $$

BRAZIL
RIO DE JANEIRO
Hotel Fasano New Ipanema property; Philippe Starck-designed interiors have a Midcentury Modern vibe. 80 Avda. Vieira Souto; 55-21/3202-4254; fasano.com.br; doubles from $$$

CHILE
EASTER ISLAND
Explora en Rapa Nui, Posada de Mike Rapu Stunning 30-room retreat from the trendsetting eco-hotel company. 866/750-6699 or 56-2/206-6060; explora.com; doubles from $$$$, all-inclusive, three-night minimum

SAN PEDRO DE ATACAMA
Tierra Atacama Hotel & Spa Design-forward property in the Andean desert. 800/829-5325 or 56-2/263-0606; tierraatacama.com; doubles from $$$, all-inclusive, two-night minimum

SANTIAGO
Grand Hyatt Stylish, contemporary rooms in a 24-story tower in the residential district of Las Condes. 4601 Avda. Kennedy; 800/233-1234 or 56-2/950-1234; grand.hyatt.com; doubles from $$$

Ritz-Carlton Polished 15-story hotel with excellent business amenities in the posh El Golf neighborhood. 15 Calle el Alcade; 800/241-3333 or 56-2/470-8500; ritzcarlton.com; doubles from $$

COLOMBIA
CARTAGENA
Charleston Cartagena Former 17th-century convent; amenities include a spa and rooftop infinity pool. Centro Plaza de Santa Teresa; 57-5/664-9494; hotelescharleston.com; doubles from $$, including breakfast

El Marqués Intimate hotel in Old Town, with one of the city's best restaurants. 33-41 Calle Nuestra Señora del Carmen; 57-5/664-4438; elmarqueshotelboutique.com; doubles from $$, including breakfast

COSTA RICA
BAJOS DEL TORO
El Silencio Lodge & Spa 16-cottage jungle eco-resort. 866/446-4063 or 506/2291-3044; elsilenciolodge.com; doubles from $$, all-inclusive

GUANACASTE
Four Seasons Resort at Peninsula Papagayo Tico-style resort flanked by two beaches on a secluded peninsula. 800/332-3442 or 506/2696-0000; fourseasons.com; doubles from $$$$

Hotel Punta Islita Eco-friendly complex on a bluff overlooking a Pacific Ocean cove. 506/2231-6122; hotelpuntaislita.com; doubles from $$, including breakfast

GUATEMALA
TIKAL
La Lancha Ten casitas on Lake Petén Itzá; the latest resort from Francis Ford Coppola. 800/746-3743 or 011-501/824-4912; blancaneaux.com; doubles from $

MEXICO
ACAPULCO
Fairmont Princess Mammoth resort modeled after an Aztec pyramid with the just-opened Pearl, a lavish hotel-within-a-hotel. 800/441-1414 or 52-744/469-1000; fairmont.com; doubles from $

A beachside palapa at the CasaSandra Hotel, on Mexico's Holbox Island.

CANCÚN

Dreams Resort & Spa On Mexico's easternmost tip, a 371-acre hotel surrounded on three sides by water. 866/237-3267 or 52-998/848-7000; dreamsresorts.com; doubles from $$$, all inclusive

JW Marriott Resort & Spa Family-friendly beachfront tower with impressive service for its size. 800/228-9290 or 52-998/848-9600; marriott.com; doubles from $$

Le Meridien Resort & Spa Eight-story tower with 3 pools and recently renovated rooms. 800/543-4300 or 52-998/881-2200; starwoodhotels.com; doubles from $$

Ritz-Carlton European-style resort; a recent expansion doubled the size of its beach. 800/241-3333 or 52-998/881-0808; ritzcarlton.com; doubles from $$$

HOLBOX ISLAND

CasaSandra Hotel Beachfront inn on a mellow island. 52-984/875-2431; casasandra.com; doubles from $$

LOS CABOS

Esperanza Resort Sprawling resort overlooking

KEY TO THE PRICE ICONS **$** UNDER $250 **$$** $250–$499 **$$$** $500–$749 **$$$$** $750–$999 **$$$$$** $1,000 AND UP

the Sea of Cortés, fresh from a $10 million renovation. 866/311-2226 or 52-624/145-6400; esperanzaresort.com; doubles from $$$, including breakfast

Las Ventanas al Paraíso, A Rosewood Resort Mediterranean-style hideaway along a picturesque beach. 888/767-3966 or 52-624/144-2800; lasventanas.com; doubles from $$$

One & Only Palmilla Legendary 1956 Spanish-revival retreat on one of Cabo's few swimmable beaches. 866/552-0001 or 52-624/146-7000; oneandonlyresorts.com; doubles from $$$

MAZATLÁN
Melville Suites Whimsical interiors (steamer-trunk tables, local folk art) in a former convent. 52-669/982-8474; themelville.com; doubles from $, including breakfast

MEXICO CITY
Four Seasons Hotel Colonial-style hacienda with world-class service and a central location. 500 Paseo de la Reforma; 800/332-3442 or 52-55/5230-1818; fourseasons.com; doubles from $$

OAXACA
Camino Real Historic hotel in a converted 16th-century convent. 800/722-6466 or 52-951/501-6100; camino-real-oaxaca.com; doubles from $$, including breakfast, three-night minimum

PUNTA MITA
Four Seasons Resort Tiled-roof casitas on an isthmus outside Puerto Vallarta, plus a new Jack Nicklaus-designed golf course. 800/332-3442 or 52-329/291-6000; fourseasons.com; doubles from $$$

RIVIERA MAYA
Mandarin Oriental Chic new villas and an excellent spa that raise the bar for high-end area resorts. 800/526-6566 or 52-984/877-3269; mandarinoriental.com; doubles from $$$

Maroma Resort & Spa Hacienda-style hotel that showcases Mayan culture. 866/454-9351 or 52-998/872-8200; maromahotel.com; doubles from $$$, including breakfast

Occidental Royal Hideaway Playacar Colonial-style villas 5 minutes from downtown Playa del Carmen. 800/999-9182 or 52-984/873-4500; royalhideaway.com; doubles from $$, all-inclusive

The Tides Collection of large rattan-and-wood villas near Playa del Carmen, in a unique jungle-and-seaside setting. 800/578-0281 or 52-984/877-3000; tidesrivieramaya.com; doubles from $$$

ZIHUATANEJO
La Casa Que Canta Adobe hideaway hugging the cliffs above Zihuatanejo Bay. 888/523-5050 or 52-755/555-7000; lacasaquecanta.com; doubles from $$

The Tides Thatched-roof palapas and stylish villas on a serene stretch of Playa la Ropa. 866/905-9560 or 52-755/555-5500; tideszihuatanejo.com; doubles from $$$

NICARAGUA
SAN JUAN DEL SUR
Morgan's Rock Hacienda & Eco-lodge Cathedral-ceilinged resort built from responsibly harvested woods; activities range from kayaking to community outreach. 506-2/232-6449; morgansrock.com; doubles from $$$, including meals

PANAMA
PANAMA CITY
Bristol Hotel Colonial property in the heart of the financial district. Avda. Aquilino de la Guardia;

011-507/265-7844; thebristol.com; doubles from $$

PERU
CUZCO
Hotel Monasterio Onetime 16th-century Spanish colonial seminary transformed by Orient-Express Hotels. 800/237-1236 or 51-84/604-000; monasteriohotel.com; doubles from $$$

LIMA
JW Marriott Hotel Modern glass tower in Miraflores's Grand Cliffs neighborhood. 615 Malecón de la Reserva; 800/228-9290 or 51-1/217-7000; jwmarriottlima.com; doubles from $$

Miraflores Park Hotel 11-story building in upscale Miraflores, steps from the coast. 1035 Malecón de la Reserva; 800/237-1236 or 51-1/610-4000; mira-park.com; doubles from $$$

MACHU PICCHU
Inkaterra Andean-style casitas on a 12-acre reserve at the foot of Machu Picchu; renowned for its progressive sustainability programs. 800/442-5042 or 51-1/610-0400; inkaterra.com; doubles from $, including breakfast and excursions

---

KEY TO THE PRICE ICONS $ UNDER $250 $$ $250–$499 $$$ $500–$749 $$$$ $750–$999 $$$$$ $1,000 AND UP

CO. MAYO

●Edinburgh

CO. CLARE
CO. LIMERICK

●Dublin

CO. WICKLOW

●Liverpool

CO. WATERFORD
CO. KERRY

●London

Brussels ●Antwerp

Paris ●Reims

Prague ●

LOIRE VALLEY

Munich ●

Vienna

●Zürich

Salzburg ●

JURA

Interlaken ●

●St. Moritz

Velden ●

DORDOGNE

●Lake Como

●Venice

Getaria ●

Milan ●

●Portofino

St.-Tropez ●

●Monte Carlo

●Bologna

DOURO VALLEY

Île de Bendor ●

●Florence

Cortona ●

Madrid ●

●Barcelona

Rome ●

SARDINIA

ANDALUSIA

AMALFI COAST
CILENTO COAST

EUROPE

AUSTRIA

SALZBURG

Hotel Goldener Hirsch
15th-century Old Town property with antique pine furnishings. 37 Getreidegasse; 800/325-3589 or 43-662/80840; goldenerhirsch.com; doubles from $$$

VELDEN

Schloss Velden 1890 château and contemporary glass-walled annex on Lake Wöerth. 877/247-6688 or 43-4274/520-000; schlossveldencapella.com; doubles from $$$

VIENNA

Hotel Bristol Grand
Opulent 19th-century hotel with an excellent restaurant, Korso bei der Oper. 1 Kärntner Ring; 800/228-3000 or 43-1/515-160; westin.com; doubles from $$$$

Palais Coburg 1840's former palace turned 35-suite hotel. 4 Coburg-bastei; 800/735-2478 or 43-1/518-180; palais-coburg.com; doubles from $$$

BELGIUM

ANTWERP

Room National Tiny, stylish B&B in the heart of the city, near museums and shopping. 24 National-estraat; 32-3/226-0700; roomnational.com; doubles from $, including breakfast

BRUSSELS

Hotel Amigo Flemish-style red-brick hotel with understated yet luxurious interiors, steps from Grand Place square. 1–3 Rue de l'Amigo; 800/223-6800 or 32-2/547-4747; hotelamigo.com; doubles from $$$$

CZECH REPUBLIC

PRAGUE

Four Seasons Hotel
Complex of interconnected Baroque, Neoclassical, and Renaissance buildings. 2A/1098 Veleslavinova; 800/332-3442 or 420-2/2142-7000; fourseasons.com; doubles from $$$

Hilton Old Town Recently refreshed property with Alexandra Champalimaud interiors. 7 V Celnici; 800/445-8667 or 420-2/2484-2364; hilton.com; doubles from $$

ENGLAND

LIVERPOOL

Hope Street Hotel Loftlike rooms in a converted 19th-century commercial building. 40 Hope St.; 44-151/709-3000; hopestreethotel.co.uk; doubles from $$

Malmaison Glass-and-steel structure on the River Mersey, near museums and historic dockyards. 7 William Jessop Way; 44-151/229-5000; malmaison.com; doubles from $

LONDON

Claridge's Landmark Mayfair hotel famed for its Gordon Ramsay restaurant and David Linley–designed suites. Brook St.; 800/637-2869 or 44-20/7589-5171; claridges.co.uk; doubles from $$$$

The Dorchester Art Deco hotel in Mayfair with a restaurant from Alain Ducasse. Park Lane; 800/650-1842 or 44-20/7629-8888; thedorchester.com; doubles from $$$$

Haymarket Hotel Theater district property from design wiz Kit Kemp. 1 Suffolk Place; 44-20/7470-4000; haymarkethotel.com; doubles from $$

Knightsbridge Hotel Clubby, contemporary feel in upscale shopping district. 10 Beaufort Gardens; 800/553-6674 or 44-20/7584-6300; knightsbridgehotel.com; doubles from $$

Mandarin Oriental Hyde Park Majestic 1889 hotel and the city's best spa. 66 Knightsbridge; 800/526-6566 or 44-20/7235-2000; mandarinoriental.com; doubles from $$$$

FRANCE

DORDOGNE

Château Les Merles
19th-century château updated by Dutch decorator Joris Van Grinsven. Tuilières; 33-5/53-63-13-42; lesmerles.com; doubles from $

ÎLE DE BENDOR

Le Delos 1962 inn built by pastis magnate Paul Ricard. 33-4/97-05-90-90; bendor.com; doubles from $$

JURA

Château de Germigney
Former marquis's estate surrounded by gardens. 33-3/84-73-85-85; chateaudegermigney.com; doubles from $

LOIRE VALLEY

Domaine des Hauts de Loire 19th-century manor in a wooded park between Blois and Amboise. Onzain; 800/735-2478 or 33-2/54-20-72-57; domainehautsloire.com; doubles from $

PARIS

Four Seasons Hotel George V Ornate 1928 landmark with Eiffel Tower views. 31 Ave. George V; 800/332-3442 or 33-1/49-52-70-00; fourseasons.com; doubles from $$$$$

KEY TO THE PRICE ICONS $ UNDER $250 $$ $250–$499 $$$ $500–$749 $$$$ $750–$999 $$$$$ $1,000 AND UP

Housekeeping staff at the Ritz, in Paris.

Hôtel Particulier Montmartre Five-room hideaway with edgy interiors. 23 Junot Ave.; 33-1/53-41-81-40; hotel-particulier-montmartre.com; doubles from $$$

Le Meurice Parisian grande dame recently refreshed by Philippe Starck. 228 Rue de Rivoli; lemeurice.com; 800/650-1842 or 33-1/44-58-10-10; doubles from $$$$

Park Hyatt Paris-Vendôme Contemporary 6-story hotel with chic interiors. 5 Rue de la Paix; 800/223-1234 or 33-1/58-71-12-34; parkhyatt.com; doubles from $$$$$

The Ritz Historic manse within walking distance of the Louvre. 15 Place Vendôme; 800/223-6800 or 33-1/43-16-30-30; ritzparis.com; doubles from $$$$$

REIMS
Château Les Crayères Turn-of-the-20th-century château in the heart of the Champagne region. 800/735-2478 or 33-3/26-82-80-80; lescrayeres.com; doubles from $$

ST.-TROPEZ
Les Palmiers 25-room hotel, a quick stroll from the Old Port. 33-4/94-97-01-61; hotel-les-palmiers.com; doubles from $

GERMANY
MUNICH
Charles Hotel Stately, cosmopolitan property inspired by Belle Époque hotels. 28 Sophienstrasse; 800/667-9477 or 49-98/544-5550; roccoforte collection.com; doubles from $$

GREECE
ATHENS
Hotel Grande Bretagne Lavishly updated 1874 hotel across from the Parliament. Constitution Square; 800/325-3589 or 30-210/333-0000; grandbretagne.gr; doubles from $$$$

King George Palace Neoclassical hotel with individually decorated rooms and views of the Acropolis. 3 Vas. Georgiou A' St.; 800/223-6800 or 30-210/322-2210;

KEY TO THE PRICE ICONS $ UNDER $250 $$ $250-$499 $$$ $500-$749 $$$$ $750-$999 $$$$$ $1,000 AND UP

kinggeorgepalace.com;
doubles from $$$$

SANTORINI
**Mystique, A Luxury
Collection Hotel** Chic
18-room cliffside property
overlooking Santorini's
caldera. 800/325-3589 or
30-22/8607-1114; mystique.
gr; doubles from $$$$

HUNGARY
BUDAPEST
**Four Seasons Hotel
Gresham Palace** Restored
Art Nouveau palace with a
glass-domed lobby. 5-6
Roosevelt Tér; 800/332-
3442 or 36-1/268-6000;
fourseasons.com; doubles
from $$

**Kempinski Hotel
Corvinus** Business-
friendly glass-and-steel
high-rise with modern
art-centric interiors,
including a gallery of
Hungarian paintings.
7-8 Erzsébet Tér; 800/
426-3135 or 36-1/429-
3777; kempinski-budapest.
com; doubles from $$

IRELAND
CO. CLARE
Dromoland Castle
16th-century baronial
manor on the edge of
Lough Dromoland.
Newmarket-on-Fergus;
353-61/368-144; dromo
land.ie; doubles from $$$

A view of
the Aegean
from the lounge
of Santorini's
Mystique.

CO. KERRY
Park Hotel Kenmare
Victorian hotel on Kenmare
Bay, with the top-notch
Samas Spa. Kenmare; 800/
525-4800 or 353-64/
41200; parkkenmare.com;
doubles from $$

CO. LIMERICK
**Adare Manor Hotel & Golf
Resort** 1832 Gothic Revival
estate with ornate embellish-
ments and a Robert Trent
Jones Sr.-designed golf
course. Adare; 800/
223-6800 or 353-61/

396-566; adaremanor.com;
doubles from $$$

CO. MAYO
Ashford Castle 700-year-
old stone castle with
20th-century additions on a
lakeside estate; activities

include falconry lessons and horseback riding. Cong; 800/346-7007 or 353-94/954-6003; ashford.ie; doubles from $$$

CO. WATERFORD
Waterford Castle Hotel & Golf Resort Restored 16th-century castle with Victorian and Georgian interiors, on a private 310-acre island in the river Suir. The Island, Waterford; 353-51/878-203; waterford castle.com; doubles from $$

CO. WICKLOW
Ritz-Carlton Powerscourt Newly constructed 200-room property on the edge of a historic estate. Enniskerry; 800/241-3333 or 353-1/274-8888; ritzcarlton.com; doubles from $$

DUBLIN
Dylan Hotel Downtown hotel with a Victorian façade and cutting-edge interiors. Eastmoreland Place; 353-1/660-3000; dylan.ie; doubles from $$, including breakfast

Four Seasons Contemporary hotel with extra-large rooms in Ballsbridge, an affluent district that offers easy access to both the city and the Wicklow Mountains. Simmonscourt Rd.; 800/332-3442 or 353-1/665-

4000; fourseasons.com; doubles from $$

The Merrion Fashionable group of four Georgian town houses, plus a modern annex, across from the National Gallery. 22-26 Upper Merrion St.; 800/223-6800 or 353-1/603-0600; merrionhotel.com; doubles from $$$

Radisson SAS Royal Hotel Design-forward business hotel in a central location. Golden Lane; 800/333-3333 or 353-1/898-2900; radissonsas.com; doubles from $

ITALY
AMALFI COAST
Capri Palace Hotel & Spa Art-filled Mediterranean hotel in Anacapri. Capri; 800/223-6800 or 39-081/978-0111; capri palace.com; doubles from $$$, including breakfast

Grand Hotel Quisisana Iconic 19th-century building steeped in old-world glamour. Capri; 800/223-6800 or 39-081/837-0788; quisisana.com; doubles from $$$, including breakfast

Il San Pietro di Positano Cliff-clinging architectural wonder over a quiet Amalfi

Coast cove. Positano; 800/735-2478 or 39-089/875-455; ilsanpietro.it; doubles from $$$, including breakfast

J. K. Place Capri Crisp and refined seaside inn. Capri; 39-081/838-4001; jkcapri.com; doubles from $$$, including breakfast

Le Sirenuse 18th-century villa overlooking the sea and Positano, with impeccable service. Positano; 800/223-6800 or 39-089/875-066; sirenuse.it; doubles from $$$$, including breakfast

Palazzo Sasso 12th-century pink palazzo in a peaceful and romantic setting high above the Mediterranean. Ravello; 39-089/818-181; palazzosasso.com; doubles from $$$, including breakfast

BOLOGNA
Grand Hotel Baglioni Frescoed 18th-century palazzo and former seminary, a stone's throw from the Piazza Maggiore. 800/223-6800 or 39-051/225-445; baglionihotels.com; doubles from $$$, including breakfast

CILENTO COAST
Il Cannito Two 13th-century buildings recently opened

as a family-run inn, in a little-visited region south of the Amalfi Coast. 39-0828/196-2277; ilcannito.com; doubles from $$, including breakfast

CORTONA
Relais & Château Il Falconiere Restored villa estate on a 25-acre vineyard outside Arezzo. 800/735-2478 or 39-05/7561-2679; ilfalconiere.it; doubles from $$

FLORENCE
Grand Hotel Villa Medici Historic 18th-century palazzo near the Uffizi. 42 Via Il Prato; 800/223-6800 or 39-055/277-171; villamedicihotel.com; doubles from $$$

Westin Excelsior Near the Ponte Vecchio, 16th-century building with traditional Tuscan décor. 3 Piazza Ognissanti; 800/228-3000 or 39-055/27151; westin.com; doubles from $$$$$

LAKE COMO
Villa d'Este Regal 16th-century lakefront estate on 25 acres of parkland. 800/223-6800 or 39-031/3481; villadeste.it; doubles from $$$$, including breakfast

KEY TO THE PRICE ICONS $ UNDER $250 $$ $250-$499 $$$ $500-$749 $$$$ $750-$999 $$$$$ $1,000 AND UP

MILAN

Four Seasons Hotel Former
convent dating from the
15th century, not far from
the city's best shopping.
6-8 Via Gesù; 800/332-
3442 or 39-02/77088;
fourseasons.com; doubles
from $$$$

PORTOFINO

Grand Hotel Miramare
Early 20th-century family-
owned hotel overlooking
the sea. 800/223-6800 or
39-0185/287-013; grand
hotelmiramare.it; doubles
from $$$

ROME

Hotel Hassler Century-old
palazzo at the top of the
Spanish Steps, offering
top-notch service and
a central location for
shoppers. 6 Piazza Trinità
dei Monti; 800/223-6800
or 39-06/699-340;
hotelhassler.com; doubles
from $$$$$

St. Regis Grand Hotel 19th-
century palace designed by
César Ritz with extraordi-
nary hand-painted frescoes,
Murano chandeliers, and
butler service. 3 Via Vittorio
E. Orlando; 877/787-3447
or 39-06/47091; stregis.
com; doubles from $$$$$

SARDINIA

Hotel Cala di Volpe Storied
resort built 40 years ago by
the Aga Khan on the posh
Costa Smeralda. 800/325-
3589 or 39-078/997-6111;
luxurycollection.com;
doubles from $$$$$,
all-inclusive

VENICE

Bauer Hotel Modern
addition to the renowned
Bauer Il Palazzo (see next
entry); the tranquil,
side-canal location is two
minutes from the Piazza San
Marco. 1459 San Marco;
800/223-6800 or 39-041/
520-7022; bauerhotels.com;
doubles from $$$$$

Bauer Il Palazzo Dignified
18th-century property
with its own Grand Canal
berth, adjacent to the
Bauer Hotel (see previous
entry). 1413/D San Marco;
800/223-6800 or 39-041/
520-7022; bauerhotels.
com; doubles from $$$$$

A dining room
at Quinta
da Romaneira,
in Portugal's
Duoro Valley.

KEY TO THE PRICE ICONS $ UNDER $250 $$ $250-$499 $$$ $500-$749 $$$$ $750-$999 $$$$$ $1,000 AND UP

Hotel Gritti Palace Opulent, Renaissance-era palazzo. 2467 Campo Santa Maria Dei Giglio; 800/325-3589 or 39-041/794-611; luxurycollection.com; doubles from $$$$$

San Clemente Palace Hotel & Resort 1700's former monastery on a private island. 1 Isola di San Clemente; 800/223-6800 or 39-041/244-5001; thi-hotels.com; doubles from $$$, including breakfast

MONACO
MONTE CARLO
Hôtel de Paris Belle Époque landmark; home to Michelin 3-starred Louis XV restaurant. Place du Casino; 800/223-6800 or 377/98-06-30-00; montecarloresort.com; doubles from $$$$

POLAND
WARSAW
Le Méridien Bristol Turn-of-the-20th-century hotel with Art Nouveau details. 42/44 Krakowskie Przedmiescie; 800/543-4300 or 48-22/551-1000; starwoodhotels.com; doubles from $$

PORTUGAL
DOURO VALLEY
Quinta da Romaneira 1,000-acre riverside spread

with two renovated manor houses. Cotas; 351-25/473-2432; maisondesreves.com; doubles from $$$$$, all-inclusive

Quinta do Vallado Five-room inn on an 18th-century wine estate. Peso da Régua; 351-25/432-3147; quintadovallado.com; doubles from $, including breakfast

SCOTLAND
EDINBURGH
The Balmoral Edwardian hotel with modern interiors in the heart of Edinburgh. 1 Princes St.; 888/667-9477 or 44-131/556-2414; thebalmoralhotel.com; doubles from $$$

SPAIN
ANDALUSIA
Casa Rural el Olivar Farmhouse converted into a comfortable inn by two Belgian expats. 34/95-753-4928; casaruralelolivar.com; doubles from $

BARCELONA
Hotel Claris Centrally located hotel that blends traditional and contemporary touches. 150 Pau Claris; 800/525-4800 or 34/90-233-7294; derbyhotels.es; doubles from $$$

GETARIA
Hotel Iturregi Elegant,

8-room country inn; a good base for exploring the Basque coast. 34/94-389-6134; hoteliturregi.com; doubles from $$, including breakfast.

MADRID
Westin Palace Neoclassical hotel in a palace commissioned by King Alfonso XII. 7 Plaza de las Cortes; 800/228-3000 or 34/91-360-8000; westin.com; doubles from $$$

SWEDEN
STOCKHOLM
Clarion Hotel Sign Glass-and-granite building furnished with pieces from Scandinavian masters like Hans Wegner. 35 Östra Järnvägsgatan; 46-8/676-9800; clarionsign.com; doubles from $$

Grand Hôtel Historic hotel opposite the harbor and the Royal Palace. 8 S. Blasieholmshamnen; 800/223-6800 or 46-8/679-3500; grandhotel.se; doubles from $$$

SWITZERLAND
INTERLAKEN
Victoria-Jungfrau Grand Hotel & Spa Classic 1864 Beaux Arts resort in an Alpine setting. 800/223-6800 or 41-33/828-2828; victoria-jungfrau.ch; doubles from $$$

ST. MORITZ
Badrutt's Palace Hotel Grande-dame property that's still at the center of the ski town's glam social scene. 800/745-8883 or 41-81/837-1000; badruttspalace.com; doubles from $$$

ZÜRICH
Baur au Lac Family-owned 165-year-old hotel overlooking Lake Zürich. 1 Talstrasse; 800/223-6800 or 41-44/220-5020; bauraulac.ch; doubles from $$$

TURKEY
ISTANBUL
Çiragan Palace Kempinski Former imperial palace on the shores of the Bosporus. 32 Çiragan Caddesi; 800/426-3135 or 90-212/326-4646; ciraganpalace.com; doubles from $$$

Four Seasons Hotel at Sultanahmet Close to the Blue Mosque, with an unparalleled Old City location. 1 Tevkifhane Sokak; 800/332-3442 or 90-212/638-8200; fourseasons.com; doubles from $$$

Swissôtel, The Bosphorus Hilltop hotel in a quiet quarter behind Dolmabahçe Palace. 2 Bayildim Caddesi Maçka; 800/223-6800 or 90-212/326-1100; swissotel.com; doubles from $$$

KEY TO THE PRICE ICONS $ UNDER $250 $$ $250–$499 $$$ $500–$749 $$$$ $750–$999 $$$$$ $1,000 AND UP

Marrakesh •

Jerusalem •

Cairo •

Doha •

• Laikipia Plateau
• Nanyuki
MASAI MARA NATIONAL RESERVE———— • ———————OL PEJETA CONSERVANCY
SERENGETI NATIONAL PARK————— • Nairobi
———AMBOSELI NATIONAL PARK
Ngorongoro Crater ————— • • Lake Manyara

• Nosy Komba
• Menabe Sakalava

Victoria Falls • ——————

ONGUMA PLAINS ————————

Benguerra
• Island
• Isalo

KRUGER NATIONAL PARK AREA ——————
MADIKWE PRIVATE GAME RESERVE ————— • Johannesburg

Oudtshoorn •
Cape Town • • Knysna

AFRICA
+ THE MIDDLE EAST

EGYPT
CAIRO
JW Marriott Hotel Business-friendly resort with golf course. Ring Rd., Mirage City; 800/228-9290 or 20-2/2411-5588; jwmarriott.com; doubles from $$

Mena House Oberoi Palace-like 1869 hotel on 40 acres, in the shadow of the Pyramids. 6 Pyramids Rd., Giza; 800/562-3764 or 20-2/3377-3222; oberoimenahouse.com; doubles from $

ISRAEL
JERUSALEM
King David Hotel 1930's property with interiors recently redone by Adam Tihany. 23 King David St.; 800/223-7773 or 972-2/620-8888; danhotels.com; doubles from $$$, including breakfast

KENYA
AMBOSELI NATIONAL PARK
Amboseli Serena Safari Lodge Red-hued lodge inspired by traditional Masai architecture. 254-20/284-2000; serena hotels.com; doubles from $$, including meals

Tortilis Camp Cluster of luxe eco-friendly tents facing Mount Kilimanjaro. 254-20/603-090; cheli

peacock.com; doubles from $$$$, all-inclusive

LAIKIPIA PLATEAU
Il Ngwesi Group Ranch & Lodge Former cattle ranch turned safari outpost and wildlife sanctuary, owned by members of the Masai tribe. 254-64/31405; lewa.org; doubles from $$$$, all-inclusive

MASAI MARA NATIONAL RESERVE
Fairmont Mara Safari Club Series of tents on the Mara River, a popular hippo watering hole. 800/257-7544 or 254-20/221-6940; fairmont.com; doubles from $$$, all-inclusive

Kichwa Tembo Pair of retro-styled tented camps overlooking the Mara Plains (*Out of Africa* was filmed here). 888/882-3742 or 27-11/809-4300; andbeyond.com; doubles from $$$$$, all-inclusive

NAIROBI
Fairmont the Norfolk Hotel The city's best hotel, complete with a formal tea-room. 800/257-7544 or 254-20/216-940; fairmont.com; doubles from $$, including breakfast

NANYUKI
Fairmont Mount Kenya Safari Club 1950's-era

hunting lodge with a genteel atmosphere, in the Mount Kenya foothills. 800/257-7544 or 254-20/216-940; fairmont.com; doubles from $$, all-inclusive

OL PEJETA CONSERVANCY
Sweetwaters Tented Camp Collection of 39 thatched-roof huts on a 90,000-acre landscaped private reserve. 254-62/32409; serena hotels.com; doubles from $$, including meals

MADAGASCAR
ISALO
Relais de la Reine Stone cottages and an excellent spa near the escarpment of Isalo National Park. 261-20/223-3623; doubles from $

NOSY KOMBA
Tsara Komba Lodge Eight private oceanfront villas with an unplugged vibe. 261-32/074-4040; tsara komba.com; doubles from $$$, including meals

MENABE SAKALAVA
Anjajavy l'Hôtel Two-story villas on a lush and remote peninsula. 33-1/4469-1500; anjajavy.com; doubles from $$$$$, 3-night minimum

MOROCCO
MARRAKESH
Angsana Riads Collection Seven private houses

converted to guest quarters, scattered throughout the city. 800/591-0439 or 65/6849-5788; angsana.com; doubles from $$

Riad Meriem Five-room sanctuary from New York designer Thomas Hays. 97 Derb El Cadi, Azbezt; 212-24/387-731; riad meriem.com; doubles from $, including breakfast

MOZAMBIQUE
BENGUERRA ISLAND
Azura Retreat Eco-resort with 15 thatched bunga-lows, each with a private plunge pool and butler. 27-11/258-0180; azura-retreats.com; doubles from $$$$$, all-inclusive, 2-night minimum

NAMIBIA
ONGUMA PLAINS
Fort on Fisher's Pan Moroccan-inspired retreat on a wildlife preserve. 264-61/232-009; onguma.com; doubles from $$$, all-inclusive

QATAR
DOHA
Sharq Village & Spa Expansive resort designed to evoke tradi-tional Qatari dwellings. Ras Abu Aboud St.; 800/241-3333 or 011-974/425-6666; sharqvillage.com; doubles from $$$

One of two guest rooms at South Africa's Boesmanskop.

SOUTH AFRICA
CAPE TOWN
Cape Grace Elegant hotel on the Victoria & Alfred Waterfront with recently refreshed rooms. Quay West Rd.; 800/223-6800 or 27-21/410-7100; capegrace.com; doubles from $$$, including breakfast

Mount Nelson Hotel Colonial 1899 property on a 9-acre estate in Cape Town's cultural center. 76 Orange St.; 800/237-1236 or 27-21/483-1000; mountnelson.co.za; doubles from $$$, including breakfast

JOHANNESBURG
Grace in Rosebank Intimately scaled hotel in the affluent suburb of Rosebank. 54 Bath Ave.; 27-11/280-7200; thegrace.co.za; doubles from $$, including breakfast

The Westcliff Nine Tuscan-inspired villas set above Westcliff Ridge. 67 Jan Smuts Ave.; 800/237-1236 or 27-11/481-6000; westcliff.co.za; doubles from $$, including breakfast

KNYSNA
Pezula Resort Hotel & Spa Enclave of 78 suites in a new oceanside development with an 18-hole golf course and horse stables. Lagoon View Dr.; 27-44/302-3333; pezularesorthotel.com; doubles from $$$

KRUGER NATIONAL PARK AREA
Singita Sabi Sand Five lodges scattered around Kruger National Park and the adjacent Sabi Sand Wildtuin; exceptional interiors, food, and service. 27-21/683-3424; singita.com; doubles from $$$$$, all-inclusive

Sabi Sabi Private Game Reserve Four diverse lodges—ranging from colonial to contemporary—in a classic bush setting. 27-11/447-7172; sabisabi.com; doubles from $$$$, all-inclusive

MADIKWE PRIVATE GAME RESERVE
Madikwe Safari Lodge Three-camp complex in the middle of a 185,000-acre wildlife preserve. 88/882-3742; andbeyond.com; doubles from $$$$$, all-inclusive

OUDTSHOORN
Boesmanskop Two-bedroom inn on an ancestral farm, filled with Cape Dutch antiques. 27-44/213-3365; boesmanskop.co.za; doubles from $ including breakfast and dinner

TANZANIA
LAKE MANYARA
Lake Manyara Serena Safari Lodge Circular, thatched-roof buildings on a lake famous for bird-watching. 255-27/280-4058 or 255-27/253-9161; serenahotels.com; doubles from $$$, including meals

NGORONGORO CRATER
Ngorongoro Crater Lodge Stilted huts with chic interiors, overlooking a 3 million-year-old caldera. 888/882-3742 or 27-11/809-4300; andbeyond.com; doubles from $$$$$, all-inclusive

Ngorongoro Serena Safari Lodge Eco-retreat carved into the crater rim, with prehistoric wall motifs, Masai carvings, and spacious rooms. 255-27/250-4058 or 255-27/253-7052; serenahotels.com; doubles from $$$, including meals

Ngorongoro Sopa Lodge Family-friendly compound with unparalleled views of the volcanic highlands. 255-27/2500-6309; sopalodges.com; doubles from $$, all-inclusive

SERENGETI NATIONAL PARK
Kirawira Luxury Tented Camp Edwardian-style encampment with period details (vintage cameras, gramophones). 255-28/262-1518; serenahotels.com; doubles from $$$$$, all-inclusive

Serengeti Serena Safari Lodge Masai-style rondavels ideally located for witnessing the wildebeest migration. 255-27/250-4058 or 255-28/262-1519; serenahotels.com; doubles from $$$, including meals

Serengeti Sopa Lodge Secluded outpost with verandas for animal sightings (year-round water holes are on the property). 255-27/2500-6309; sopalodges.com; doubles from $$, all-inclusive

ZAMBIA
VICTORIA FALLS
Royal Livingstone Gracious hotel in colonial-style buildings on Victoria Falls. 800/223-6800 or 27-11/780-7800; suninternational.com; doubles from $$$$, including breakfast

ZIMBABWE
VICTORIA FALLS
Victoria Falls Hotel 1904 hotel in Victoria Falls National Park, a 10-minute walk along a private footpath from the cascades. 800/745-8883 or 263-13/44751; victoriafallshotel.com; doubles from $$, including breakfast

KEY TO THE PRICE ICONS $ UNDER $250 $$ $250-$499 $$$ $500-$749 $$$$ $750-$999 $$$$$ $1,000 AND UP

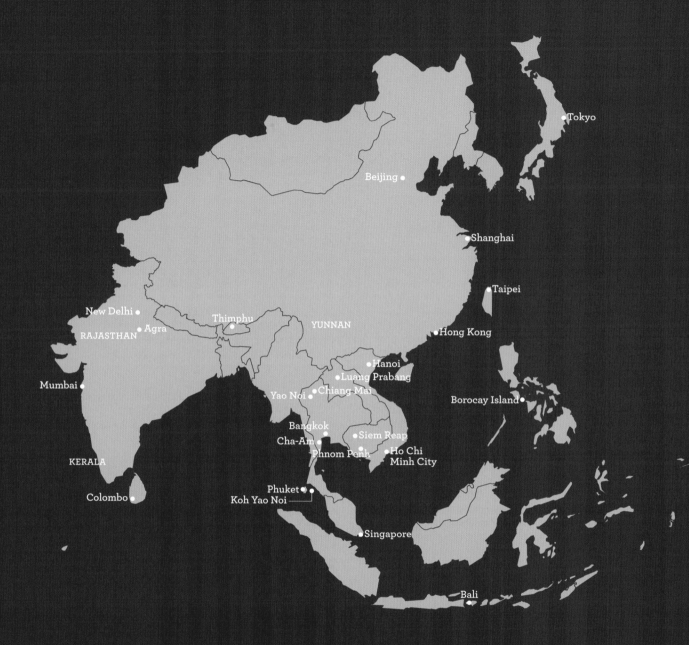

New Delhi
RAJASTHAN
Agra
Thimphu
YUNNAN
Beijing
Shanghai
Taipei
Tokyo
Hong Kong
Hanoi
Luang Prabang
Yao Noi
Chiang Mai
Mumbai
Bangkok
Cha-Am
Siem Reap
Borocay Island
Phnom Penh
Ho Chi
Minh City
KERALA
Phuket
Colombo
Koh Yao Noi
Singapore
Bali

ASIA

BHUTAN
THIMPHU
Taj Tashi The country's first upscale city property; interiors are inspired by traditional Buddhist art. Samtem Lam, Chubachu; 866/969-1825 or 97-52/336-699; tajhotels.com; doubles from $$

CAMBODIA
PHNOM PENH
Raffles Hotel Le Royal Centrally located 1920's French colonial mansion that's home to one of the city's best restaurants. 92 Rukhak Vithei Daun Penh; 800/768-9009 or 855-23/981-888; raffles.com; doubles from $$

SIEM REAP
Raffles Grand Hotel d'Angkor Restored 1932 hotel in the heart of town—a perfect base for exploring Angkor Wat. 800/768-9009 or 855-63/963-888; raffles.com; doubles from $$

CHINA
BEIJING
China World Hotel Elliptical building with sumptuous interiors in the central business district. 1 Jian Guo Men Wai Rd.; 866/565-5050 or 86-10/6505-2266; shangri-la.com; doubles from $$, including breakfast

Grand Hyatt Modern, business-friendly hotel steps from the Wangfujing metro station. 1 E. Chang An Ave.; 800/233-1234 or 86-10/8518-1234; grand.hyatt.com; doubles from $$

Park Hyatt Soaring 237-room hotel on the top 19 floors of the city's tallest tower. 2 Jian Guo Men Wai Rd.; 800/233-1234 or 86-10/8567-1234; parkhyatt.com; doubles from $$

Peninsula Beijing Opulent property that mixes traditional Chinese aesthetics with of-the-moment amenities such as a holistic spa; a 20-minute walk from the Forbidden City and Tiananmen Square. 8 Goldfish Lane; 866/382-8388 or 86-10/8516-2888; peninsula.com; doubles from $$, including breakfast

Ritz-Carlton The company's second Beijing property, in the emerging Chaoyang District, known for excellent shopping. 83A Jian Guo Rd.; 800/241-3333 or 86-10/5908-8888; ritzcarlton.com; doubles from $$$

Shangri-La Hotel Landmark building set in scenic gardens near the Financial District; some of the city's largest standard rooms (540 square feet in the Valley Wing). 29 Zizhuyuan Rd.; 866/565-5050 or 86-10/6841-2211; shangri-la.com; doubles from $$, including breakfast

St. Regis Hotel High-rise hotel in the Jian Guo Men Wai business district; recently reopened following a $27 million renovation. 21 Jian Guo Men Wai Rd.; 877/787-3447 or 86-10/6460-6688; stregis.com; doubles from $$$

HONG KONG
Conrad Business hotel on floors 40-61 of the Pacific Place towers, near the MTR and convention center. 88 Queensway; 800/266-7237 or 852/2521-3838; conradhotels.com; doubles from $$$

Four Seasons Hotel Stylish, contemporary waterfront hotel in an unparalleled Central location; rooms are spread over two towers. 8 Finance St.; 800/332-3442 or 852/3196-8888; fourseasons.com; doubles from $$$

Grand Hyatt Lavish waterfront property near the convention center, with an expansive fitness complex (1,312-foot running track, driving range). 1 Harbour Rd.; 800/233-1234 or 852/2588-1234; grand.hyatt.com; doubles from $$$

InterContinental Kowloon waterfront tower that houses two of Hong Kong's most favored dining outposts—Nobu and Alain Ducasse's Spoon. 18 Salisbury Rd.; 800/327-0200 or 852/2721-1211; intercontinental.com; doubles from $$$

JW Marriott Hotel Popular business hotel in Pacific Place with newly redone guest rooms. 88 Queensway; 800/228-9290 or 852/2810-8366; jwmarriott.com; doubles from $$$

Kowloon Shangri-La Grand hotel set in Kowloon's Tsim Sha Tsui, with a stunning two-story lobby and floor-to-ceiling windows in every guest room. 64 Mody Rd.; 866/565-5050 or 852/2721-2111; shangri-la.com; doubles from $$

Luxe Manor Eccentric Dalí-inspired hotel in the Tsim Sha Tsui district. 39 Kimberley Rd.; 852/3763-8888; theluxemanor.com; doubles from $$

The lobby lounge at the Banyan Tree Lijiang, in Yunnan, China.

Mandarin Oriental Hong Kong institution where legendary service meets modern refinement, in the heart of Central. 5 Connaught Rd.; 800/526-6566 or 852/2522-0111; mandarinoriental.com; doubles from $$$

Peninsula Hong Kong Iconic 1928 Neoclassical-style hotel overlooking Victoria Harbour. Salisbury Rd.; 866/382-8388 or 852/2920-2888; peninsula. com; doubles from $$$

SHANGHAI
Four Seasons Hotel Tower with European-style interiors, located near People's Square and Nanjing Road. 500 Weihai Rd.; 800/332-3442 or 86-21/6256-8888; fourseasons.com; doubles from $$$

Grand Hyatt Floors 53–87 in the landmark 88-story Jin Mao Tower, in the Pudong Lujiazui financial district. 88 Century Blvd.; 800/233-1234 or 86-21/5049-1234; grand.hyatt. com; doubles from $$$

Jia Trendy 55-room property; interiors were designed by a team of cutting-edge artists. 931 Nanjing Xi Rd.; 86-21/6217-9000; jiashanghai. com; doubles from $$

JW Marriott Hotel at Tomorrow Square The top floors of a 60-story shopping and business complex, centrally located opposite People's Square. 399 Nanjing Xi Rd.; 800/228-9290 or 86-21/5359-4969; jwmarriott.com; doubles from $$

Portman Ritz-Carlton Fifty-story high-rise near the Shanghai Exhibition Center; the business center has just been redone. 1376 Nanjing Xi Rd.; 800/241-3333 or 86-21/6279-8888; ritzcarlton.com; doubles from $$$

Pudong Shangri-La Pair of towers on the eastern bank of the Huangpu River, in central Pudong. 33 Fu Cheng Rd.; 866/565-5050 or 86-21/6882-8888; shangri-la. com; doubles from $$

St. Regis Hotel Elegant red-granite building in Pudong, with ultra-personal service (thanks to the white-gloved butlers). 889 Dong Fang Rd.; 877/787-3447 or 86-21/5050-4567; stregis. com; doubles from $$

Urbn Sustainably minded new property from China's first green-conscious hotel group. 183 Jiao Zhou Rd.; 86-21/5153-4600; urbn hotels.com; doubles from $

Westin Bund Center Two 26-story towers with contemporary interiors and an impressive art collection, a five-minute walk from the Bund. 88 Henan Central Rd.; 800/228-3000 or 86-21/6335-1888; westin. com; doubles from $$$

YUNNAN
Banyan Tree Lijiang Traditional curved-roof villas set amid gardens and pools. 800/591-0439 or 86-88/8533-1111; banyan tree.com; doubles from $$$

INDIA
AGRA
Oberoi Amarvilas Contemporary Moorish- and Mughal-inspired fantasy of marble pools and fountains; each room has a Taj Mahal view. 800/562-3764 or 91-562/233-1515; oberoiamarvilas. com; doubles from $$$

KERALA
Kumarakom Lake Resort Lakeside cottages inspired by regional architecture, set on a canal-shaped pool. Kottayam; 800/425-5030 or 91-48/1252-4900; klresort.com; doubles from $$, including breakfast, two-night minimum

MUMBAI
Taj Mahal Palace & Tower 1903 grand hotel plus a modern tower, overlooking the Gateway of India. Apollo Bunder; 866/969-1825 or 91-22/6665-3366; tajhotels.com; doubles from $$, including breakfast

NEW DELHI
The Imperial Art Deco landmark steps from Connaught Place, with old-world charm and a fantastic art collection. Janpath; 800/323-7500 or 91-11/2334-1234; theimperialindia.com; doubles from $$

The Oberoi Business hotel a short walk from Pragati Maidan, with a glamorous restaurant and bar scene, and the first-rate Banyan Tree spa. Dr. Zakir Hussain Marg; 800/562-3764 or 91-11/2436-3030; oberoidelhi.com; doubles from $$

Taj Mahal Hotel Contemporary business hotel in the upscale Lutyens' Delhi neighborhood. 1 Mansingh Rd.; 866/969-1825 or 91-11/2302-6162; tajhotels. com; doubles from $$, including breakfast

KEY TO THE PRICE ICONS $ UNDER $250 $$ $250–$499 $$$ $500–$749 $$$$ $750–$999 $$$$$ $1,000 AND UP

The sitting room in a lofted guest suite at Singapore's New Majestic.

RAJASTHAN

Oberoi Rajvilas
Rajasthani-style fortress with luxury tents and villas. Jaipur; 800/562-3764 or 91-141/268-0101; oberoirajvilas.com; doubles from $$$

Oberoi Udaivilas Impeccable lakeside palace of marble, sandstone, and gold leaf, on former royal hunting grounds. Udaipur; 800/562-3764 or 91-294/243-3300; oberoiudaivilas.com; doubles from $$$

Rambagh Palace Former royal guesthouse and hunting lodge, with an excellent new spa. Jaipur; 866/969-1825 or 91-141/221-1919; tajhotels.com; doubles from $$$, including breakfast

Samode Palace Historic Rajput-Moghal estate with 43 light-filled rooms. Samode; 800/323-7500 or 91-142/324-0013; preferredhotels.com; doubles from $

Taj Lake Palace Fairy-tale centuries-old palace rising from its own island in the middle of Lake Pichola. Udaipur; 866/969-1825 or 91-294/242-8800; tajhotels.

com; doubles from $$$, including breakfast

Umaid Bhawan Palace Magnificent Art Deco-inspired hotel from the Taj group, in a striking 1930's building. Jodhpur; 866/969-1825 or 91-291/251- 0101; tajhotels. com; doubles from $$$$

INDONESIA
BALI
Amankila Freestanding suites on a jungly slope, with private terraces and a triple-tiered pool overlooking the Lombok Strait. 800/477-9180 or 62-363/41-333; amanresorts.com; doubles from $$$$

Hotel Tugu Bali Intimate beachfront hotel filled with the owner's Asian antiques. 800/225-4255 or 62-361/731-701; tuguhotels.com; doubles from $$

Sentosa Stylish villas with kitchens and a buzzed-about restaurant, Blossom. 866/491-8372 or 62-361/730-333; balisentosa.com; villas from $$$

JAPAN
TOKYO
Imperial Hotel Legendary 119-year-old hotel with superb business facilities in a prime location near the Imperial Palace. 1-1 Uchisaiwai-cho 1-chome; 800/223-6800 or 81-3/3504-1111; imperialhotel.co.jp; doubles from $$

Park Hyatt Sleek hotel on the top 14 floors of Kenzo Tange's 52-story steel-and-granite West Shinjuku tower. 3-7-1-2 Nishi-Shinjuku; 800/233-1234 or 81-3/5322-1234; park.hyatt.com; doubles from $$$

LAOS
LUANG PRABANG
La Résidence Phou Vao Sprawling resort at the edge of town, built in French colonial style, with minimalist decor and an excellent spa. 800/237-1236 or 856-71/212-194; residencephouvao.com; doubles from $$

PHILIPPINES
BORACAY ISLAND
Spider House Seven simple, thatched-roof bungalows with extraordinary sea views. 63-36/288-4568; doubles from $

SINGAPORE
SINGAPORE
The Fairmont (formerly Raffles the Plaza) Modern, polished hotel in the heart

A patio at the Mandarin Oriental, in Bangkok.

of the commercial district. 80 Bras Basah Rd.; 800/441-1414 or 65/6339-7777; fairmont.com; doubles from $$

Grand Hyatt Pair of high-rises with residential-style rooms, just off Orchard Road. 10 Scotts Rd.; 800/233-1234 or 65/6738-1234; grand.hyatt.com; doubles from $$

Mandarin Oriental Fan-shaped hotel in a bustling location adjacent to Marina Square and linked to the convention center. 5 Raffles Ave.; 800/526-6566 or 65/6338-0066; mandarinoriental.com; doubles from $$

New Majestic Eye-popping interiors designed by local artists, in a 1928 Chinatown building. 31-37 Bukit Pasoh Rd.; 800/337-4685 or 65/6511-4700; newmajestic hotel.com; doubles from $

KEY TO THE PRICE ICONS $ UNDER $250 $$ $250-$499 $$$ $500-$749 $$$$ $750-$999 $$$$$ $1,000 AND UP

Raffles Hotel Iconic hotel in an 1887 colonial-style building surrounded by tropical gardens. 1 Beach Rd.; 800/768-9009 or 65/6337-1886; raffles.com; doubles from $$$$

Ritz-Carlton, Millenia Tower surrounded by seven acres of gardens, in the Marina Bay district. 7 Raffles Ave.; 800/241-3333 or 65/6337-8888; ritzcarlton.com; doubles from $$

SRI LANKA
COLOMBO

Casa Colombo Ornate original details meet striking modern touches in this 200-year-old mansion. 231 Galle Rd., Bambalapitiya; 94-11/452-0130; casa colombo; doubles from $

TAIWAN
TAIPEI

Grand Hyatt Business-friendly hotel tower centrally located in the World Trade Centre; the new spa just opened. 2 Song Shou Rd. 800/233-1234 or 886-2/2720-1234; grand.hyatt.com; doubles from $$

THAILAND
BANGKOK

JW Marriott Hotel Modern skyscraper steps from the SkyTrain on Sukhumvit

Road (the city's restaurant and nightlife district). 4 Sukhumvit Rd., Soi 2; 800/228-9290 or 66-2/656-7700; jwmarriott.com; doubles from $$

Mandarin Oriental Landmark property just off the Chao Phraya river, known for its unmatched service and loyal staff. 48 Oriental Ave.; 800/526-6566 or 66-2/659-9000; mandarinoriental.com; doubles from $$

Peninsula Bangkok Sleek Asian-inspired interiors, excellent service, and a 19,000-square-foot spa in a 39-story tower. 333 Charoennakorn Rd.; 866/382-8388 or 66-2/861-2888; peninsula.com; doubles from $$

Royal Orchid Sheraton Hotel & Towers Colossal riverfront hotel in the commercial district, adjacent to the city's largest antiques shopping mall. 2 Charoen Krung Rd., Soi 30; 800/325-3535 or 66-2/266-0123; sheraton.com; doubles from $

Seven Contemporary, Buddhist-inspired guest rooms in a Sukhumvit neighborhood town house.

3/15 Sukhumvit Soi 31; 66-26/620-951; sleepat seven.com; doubles from $

Shangri-La Hotel Expansive two-tower complex with tropical gardens, a superb location along the Chao Phraya river, and notable amenities such as the Chi Spa. 89 Soi Wat Suan Plu, New Rd.; 866/565-5050 or 66-2/236-7777; shangri-la.com; doubles from $$

Sheraton Grande Sukhumvit Business-friendly high-rise, centrally located and connected to a SkyTrain stop, with casual yet chic rooms. 250 Sukhumvit Rd.; 800/325-3535 or 66-2/649-8888; sheraton.com; doubles from $$

CHA-AM

Alila Cha-am Streamlined oceanside hideaway in an emerging, buzzed-about beach destination. 66-32/709-555; alilahotels.com; doubles from $

CHIANG MAI

Four Seasons Resort Cluster of pavilions surrounded by rice paddies in the Mae Rim Valley, with an authentic up-country atmosphere. 800/332-3442 or 66-53/298-181; fourseasons.com; doubles from $$$

KOH YAO NOI

Six Senses Hideaway Luxury villas on a tiny isle 45 minutes from Phuket by boat. 800/591-7480 or 66-76/418-500; six-senses.com; doubles from $$$$$

PHUKET

JW Marriott Resort & Spa Family-friendly resort with 27 acres of tropical gardens and 10 miles of beachfront on the Andaman Sea. 800/228-9290 or 66-76/338-000; jwmarriott.com; doubles from $$

VIETNAM
HANOI

Sofitel Metropole A 108-year-old landmark, set between Hoan Kiem Lake and the Opera House. 15 Ngo Quyen St.; 800/763-4835 or 84-4/3826-6919; sofitel.com; doubles from $$, including breakfast

HO CHI MINH CITY

Park Hyatt Saigon French colonial–style building with refined design touches (lacquer; mother-of-pearl; dark woods), overlooking the Opera House. 2 Lam Son Square; 800/233-1234 or 84-8/3824-1234; park.hyatt.com; doubles from $$

KEY TO THE PRICE ICONS $ UNDER $250 $$ $250-$499 $$$ $500-$749 $$$$ $750-$999 $$$$$ $1,000 AND UP

A guest villa at Six Senses Hideaway, in Thailand's Phang Nga Bay.

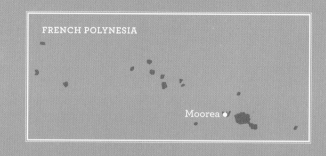

Moorea •

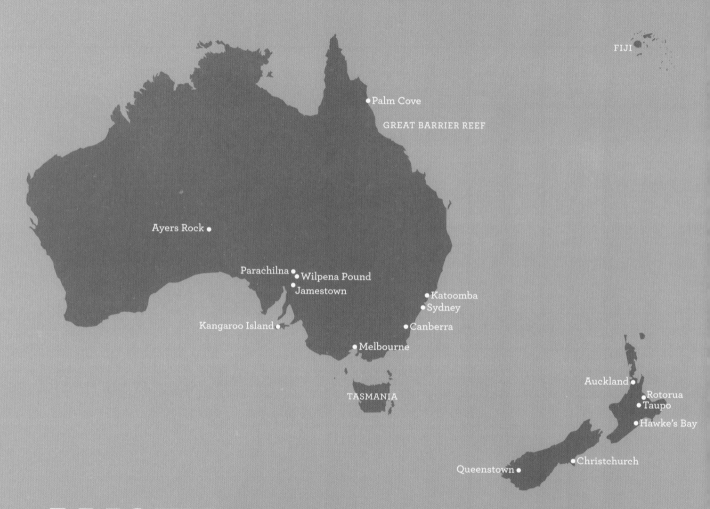

FIJI

• Palm Cove

GREAT BARRIER REEF

Ayers Rock •

Parachilna • • Wilpena Pound
• Jamestown

• Katoomba
• Sydney

Kangaroo Island • • Canberra

• Melbourne

TASMANIA

Auckland • • Rotorua
• Taupo

• Hawke's Bay

Queenstown • • Christchurch

AUSTRALIA+
NEW ZEALAND+
THE SOUTH PACIFIC

AUSTRALIA

AYERS ROCK

Voyages Longitude 131°
Palatial tents on an
isolated outback sand
dune. 61-2/8296-8010;
voyages.com.au; doubles
from $$$$, all-inclusive

CANBERRA

Diamant Hotel
Stylish new 80-room
property in an Art Deco
building. 15 Edinburgh Ave.;
61-2/6175-2222; diamant.
com.au; doubles from $

GREAT BARRIER REEF

Hayman Private 726-acre
island flanked by coral
reefs. 800/223-6800 or
61-7/4940-1234; hayman.
com.au; doubles from
$$$, including breakfast

Voyages Lizard Island
Ultra-secluded and
romantic private-island
retreat surrounded by
24 white sand beaches.
800/225-9849 or 61-2/
8296-8010; lizardisland.
com.au; doubles from
$$$$$, all-inclusive,
two-night minimum

JAMESTOWN

**North Bundaleer
Homestead** Newly
restored, rural 1901
manor house. 61-8/8665-
4024; northbundaleer.
com.au; doubles from $$,
including meals

KANGAROO ISLAND

Southern Ocean Lodge
Eco-conscious resort
on a wildlife-filled island
30 minutes by plane from
Adelaide; 21 spacious,
airy suites. 61-2/9918-
4355; southernocean
lodge.com.au; doubles
from $$$$$, all-inclusive,
two-night minimum

KATOOMBA

**Lilianfels Blue
Mountains Resort
& Spa** 1889 country
house with English
gardens and décor, on
a bluff above the
Jamison Valley. 800/
237-1236 or 61-2/
4780-1200; lilianfels.
com.au; doubles from $

MELBOURNE

Grand Hyatt Modern
Italianate high-rise
near Federation Square;
recently underwent a
$29 million renovation.
123 Collins St.; 800/
223-1234 or 61-3/
9657-1234; grand.hyatt.
com; doubles from $

The Langham
Sophisticated riverside
hotel convenient to the
arts and business districts.
1 Southgate Ave.; 800/
745-8883 or 61-3/
8696-8888; langham
hotelmelbourne.com.au;
doubles from $$

Park Hyatt Downtown
hotel with 20 floors,
Art Deco–style interiors,
and a first-rate spa.
1 Parliament Square;
800/223-1234 or 61-3/
9224-1234; park.hyatt.
com; doubles from $$

**Sofitel Melbourne
on Collins** I. M. Pei-
designed 55-story tower
with breathtaking city
views, in the heart of
the shopping and theater
districts. 25 Collins St.;
800/763-4835 or
61-3/9653-0000; sofitel
melbourne.com.au;
doubles from $$

PALM COVE

Kewarra Beach Resort
Beachfront lodge and
bungalows on tropical
grounds, near the Great
Barrier Reef. 61-7/4057-
6666; kewarra.com;
doubles from $$,
including transfers

**Sebel Reef House
& Spa** Breezy 69-room
resort with three pools
and a great spa, between
the rainforest and the
reef. 61-7/4055-3633;
reefhouse.com.au;
doubles from $$

PARACHILNA

Prairie Hotel Intimate
lodge in the outback,
with an atmospheric 1876

bar. 61-8/8648-4844;
prairiehotel.com.au;
doubles from $

SYDNEY

Four Seasons Hotel
A three-level atrium lobby
and views of the Opera
House, plus the largest
heated outdoor pool in
town. 199 George St.;
800/332-3442 or 61-2/
9250-3100; fourseasons.
com; doubles from $

InterContinental
Smartly refurbished
tower hotel with Victorian-
style interiors, steps
from the Royal Botanic
Gardens. 117 Macquarie
St.; 800/327-0200 or
61-2/9253-9000; inter
continental.com; doubles
from $$

Observatory Hotel
Just-refreshed hotel
with old-world charm
in the residential Rocks
district. 89-113 Kent St.;
800/237-1236 or 61-2/
9256-2222; observatory
hotel.com.au; doubles
from $$$

Park Hyatt Art-filled,
contemporary water-
front hotel, with unparal-
leled Sydney Harbour
views and some of the
city's largest standard
rooms. 7 Hickson Rd.;
800/233-1234 or

61-2/9241-1234; park.hyatt.com; doubles from $$

Sheraton on the Park
Downtown property next to Hyde Park, a quick walk from the harbor. 161 Elizabeth St.; 800/325-3535 or 61-2/9286-6000; starwoodhotels.com; doubles from $$

The Westin Former post office building with skyscraper annex in a central downtown location; the city's best hotel for business travelers. 1 Martin Place; 800/228-3000 or 61-2/8223-1111; westin.com.au; doubles from $$

TASMANIA
Voyages Cradle Mountain Lodge
Secluded 40-acre complex of timber cabins on the edge of Cradle Mountain–Lake St. Clair National Park. 800/225-9849 or 61-3/6492-2100; cradlemountainlodge.com.au; doubles from $, including breakfast

WILPENA POUND
Arkaba Station
Comfortable, family-run retreat on a working sheep farm. 61-8/8648-4195;

arkabastation.com; doubles from $, two-night minimum

FIJI
DENARAU ISLAND
Sheraton Fiji Resort
Recently renovated beachside complex with a family-friendly vibe and a host of water activities. 800/325-3535 or 011-679/675-0777; sheraton.com; doubles from $$

FRENCH POLYNESIA
MOOREA
InterContinental Resort & Spa Spare, airy hillside villas fronting a lagoon. 800/327-0200 or 689/604-900; intercontinental.com; doubles from $$$$

NEW ZEALAND
AUCKLAND
Hilton Gleaming white complex on Princes Wharf near the business district and Sky City Tower. 147 Quay St.; 800/445-8667 or 64-9/978-2000; hilton.com; doubles from $$

Hyatt Regency
High-rise hotel with modern interiors and superior business amenities, just minutes from the city center.

Corner of Princes St. and Waterloo Quadrant; 800/233-1234 or 64-9/355-1234; hyatt.com; doubles from $

Stamford Plaza
Well-appointed downtown hotel with views of Auckland's Waitemata Harbour. 22-24 Albert St.; 64-9/309-8888; stamford.com.au; doubles from $

CHRISTCHURCH
The George
Boutique hotel with streamlined interiors and two well-regarded restaurants, across from Hagley Park and a short drive from downtown. 50 Park Terrace; 800/525-4800 or 64-3/379-4560; thegeorge.com; doubles from $

HAWKE'S BAY
Farm at Cape Kidnappers Stylish 26-room lodge with an 18-hole golf course and one of the area's best wine cellars, on a 6,000-acre working sheep farm. 800/735-2478 or 64-6/875-1900; capekidnappers.com; doubles from $$$, all-inclusive

QUEENSTOWN
Matakauri Lodge & Spa Alpine-style

lodge and six villas along Douglas fir–lined Lake Wakatipu. 64-3/441-1008; matakauri.co.nz; doubles from $$$$, including breakfast and dinner

Millbrook Resort
Golf-focused and tree-lined villa resort with an 18-hole course and one of the country's best spas, 20 minutes from Queenstown. 64-3/441-7000; millbrook.co.nz; doubles from $

ROTORUA
Treetops Lodge & Wilderness Experience
Timber-and-stone complex with an impressive array of outdoor activities (horseback riding, fishing, kayaking), on a private 2,500-acre nature reserve. 64-7/333-2066; treetops.co.nz; doubles from $$$$, all-inclusive

TAUPO
Huka Lodge The gold standard for New Zealand lodges: an exclusive retreat on 17 breathtaking riverfront acres. 800/525-4800 or 64-7/378-5791; hukalodge.com; doubles from $$$$$, including meals

Matakauri Lodge,
on New Zealand's
Lake Wakatipu.

The pagoda
entrance to
Banyan Tree
Lijiang, in China's
Yunnan province.

TRIPS
DIRECTORY

Inside room
No. 14 at the
Horned Dorset
Primavera
in Rincón,
Puerto Rico.

INDEX

CONTRIBUTORS

Richard Alleman

Tom Austin

Tarini Awatramani

Luke Barr

Laura Begley

Thomas Beller

Andrea Bennett

Ardyn Bernoth

Ian Buruma

Sana Butler

Aric Chen

Jennifer V. Cole

Yolanda Crous

Gillian Cullinan

Anthony Dennis

Claire Downey

Matthew Evans

Amy Farley

Jennifer Flowers

Gayle Forman

Devin Friedman

Charles Gandee

Michael Gross

Darrell Hartman

Kendall Hill

Tina Isaac

Sarah Kantrowitz

Xander Kaplan

Catherine Keenan

David A. Keeps

Stirling Kelso

Chris Kucway

Daniel Kurtz-Phelan

Matt Lee

Ted Lee

Peter Jon Lindberg

Alexandra Marshall

Alex Frew McMillan

Steve Meacham

Robert Milliken

Clark Mitchell

Shane Mitchell

Monalika Namchoom

John Newton

Jane Parbury

Danielle Pergament

Christopher Petkanas

David Propson

Douglas Rogers

Frank Rose

Bruce Schoenfeld

Oliver Schwaner-Albright

Clara O. Sedlak

George Semler

Kevin Sessums

Maria Shollenbarger

Andrew Solomon

Bree Sposato

Jeff Spurrier

Melinda Stevens

Leisa Tyler

Sita Wadhwani

Jennifer Welbel

Caroline West

Sarah Wildman

Nina Willdorf

Jeff Wise

Elizabeth Woodson

Joe Yogerst

PHOTOGRAPHERS

A magazine of modern global culture,
Travel + Leisure examines the places, ideas,
and trends that define the way we travel now.
T+L inspires readers to explore the world, equipping
them with expert advice and a better understanding
of the endless possibilities of travel. Delivering clear,
comprehensive service journalism, intelligent
writing, and evocative photography, T+L is the
authority for today's traveler. Visit us at
travelandleisure.com.